Masters of Modern Art: 12 Artists and Their 56 Iconic Works

CONTENTS

Alexej von Jawlensky, 1864~1941

Alexej von Jawlensky was a Russian painter born in 1864 in Torzhok, coming from a noble background. Initially serving as an officer in the Imperial Guard, he moved to Saint Petersburg, driven by a passion for art, where he studied under the realist painter Ilja Repin. In 1896, he left Russia for Munich to pursue a career as a painter, and there he met Marianne von Werefkin, who would become his wife.

While attending the Munich Art School, Jawlensky developed a friendship with Wassily Kandinsky, which contributed to his artistic growth. In 1905, after collaborating with Henri Matisse in France, he gained new inspiration for color. He returned to Germany and immersed himself in the Expressionist movement centered in Munich. His creative work in Murnau, a small town in Bavaria, significantly influenced his artistic development.

In 1909, he founded the Neue Künstlervereinigung München (New Artist Association Munich), allowing artists to expand their networks and celebrate artistic diversity. He joined the Blaue Reiter (Blue Rider) group in 1912. However, with the outbreak of World War I in 1914, the group disbanded, marking a pivotal moment in his work. During this period, he produced landscape-themed works before focusing on semi-abstract portraiture. Jawlensky infused his frontal portraits with a sense of mystique, creating a meditative atmosphere.

In 1924, he formed the Blue Four with Kandinsky, Paul Klee, and Lyonel Feininger. He struggled with paralysis due to arthritis starting in the mid-1930s and passed away in 1941.

Meditation Yellow Head, 1936

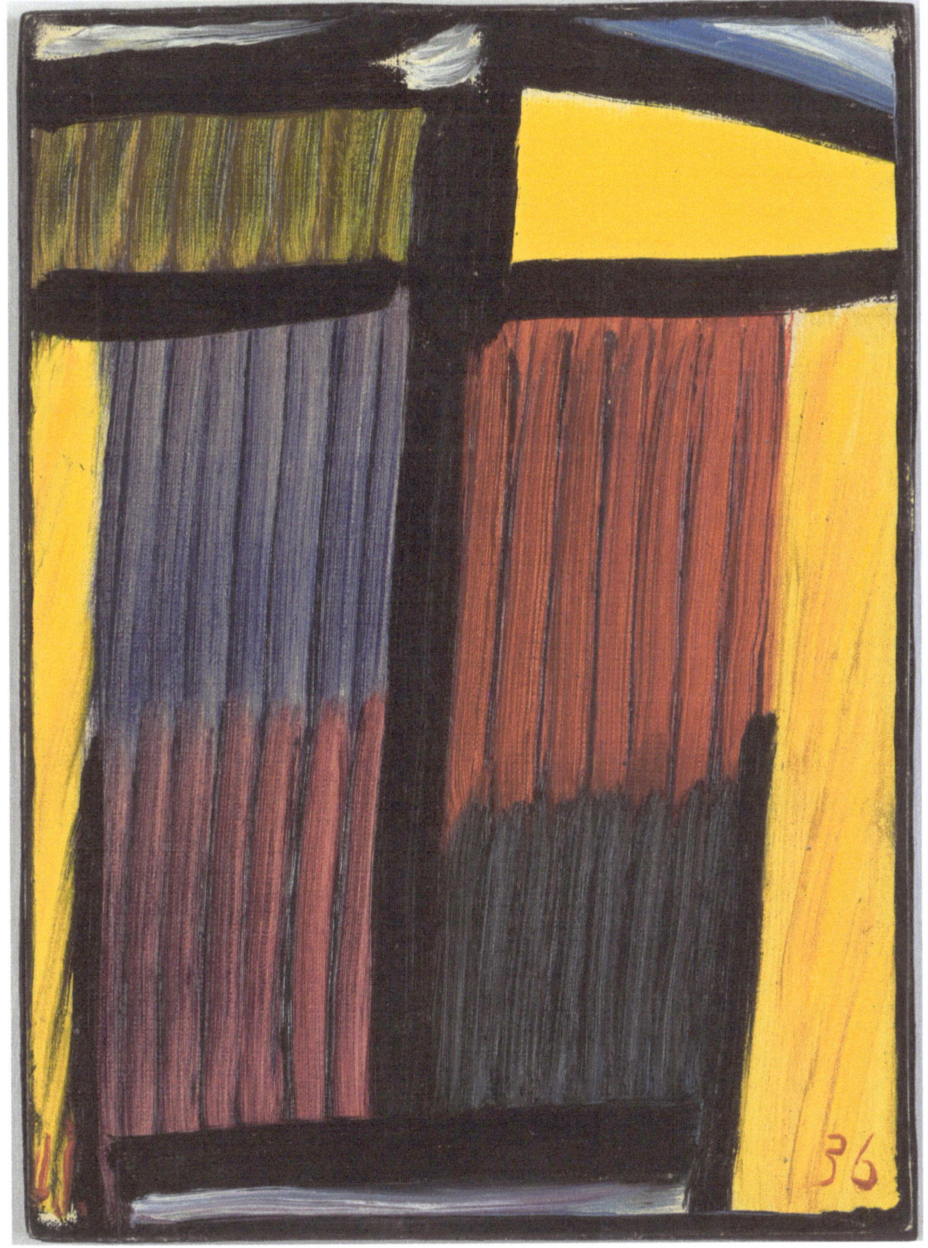

24.8 x 18.5 cm

Baroness Elsa von Freytag-Loringhoven, 1874~1927

Baroness Elsa von Freytag-Loringhoven was one of the most controversial radical female artists in the New York art scene of the early 20th century. A poet, sculptor, and performance artist originally from Germany, she was somewhat overlooked during her time but later received renewed attention.

Born in 1874 in Pomerania, Germany, she showed a passion for art and literature through various activities across Europe, gaining recognition for her creative work after moving to the United States.

In the late 1910s, while living in Greenwich Village, the hub of the New York art scene, she engaged with a diverse array of artists and writers, continuing her unique creative pursuits. She performed in public spaces wearing extravagant costumes, capturing the attention of many. Elsa was also a talented writer, and her relationship with Marcel Duchamp significantly influenced her artistic tendencies.

Duchamp's famous ready-made work, Fountain, created in 1917, featured an overturned ceramic urinal. There are claims that Elsa played a role in the creation of this piece, suggesting that her artistic style and her passion for Duchamp's innovative approach to ready-made art may have influenced its development.

Elsa's work diverged from the social and cultural norms of her time, making it difficult for her to gain full recognition. However, in the late 20th century, she began to receive renewed attention, and her impact on modernist art has since been acknowledged.

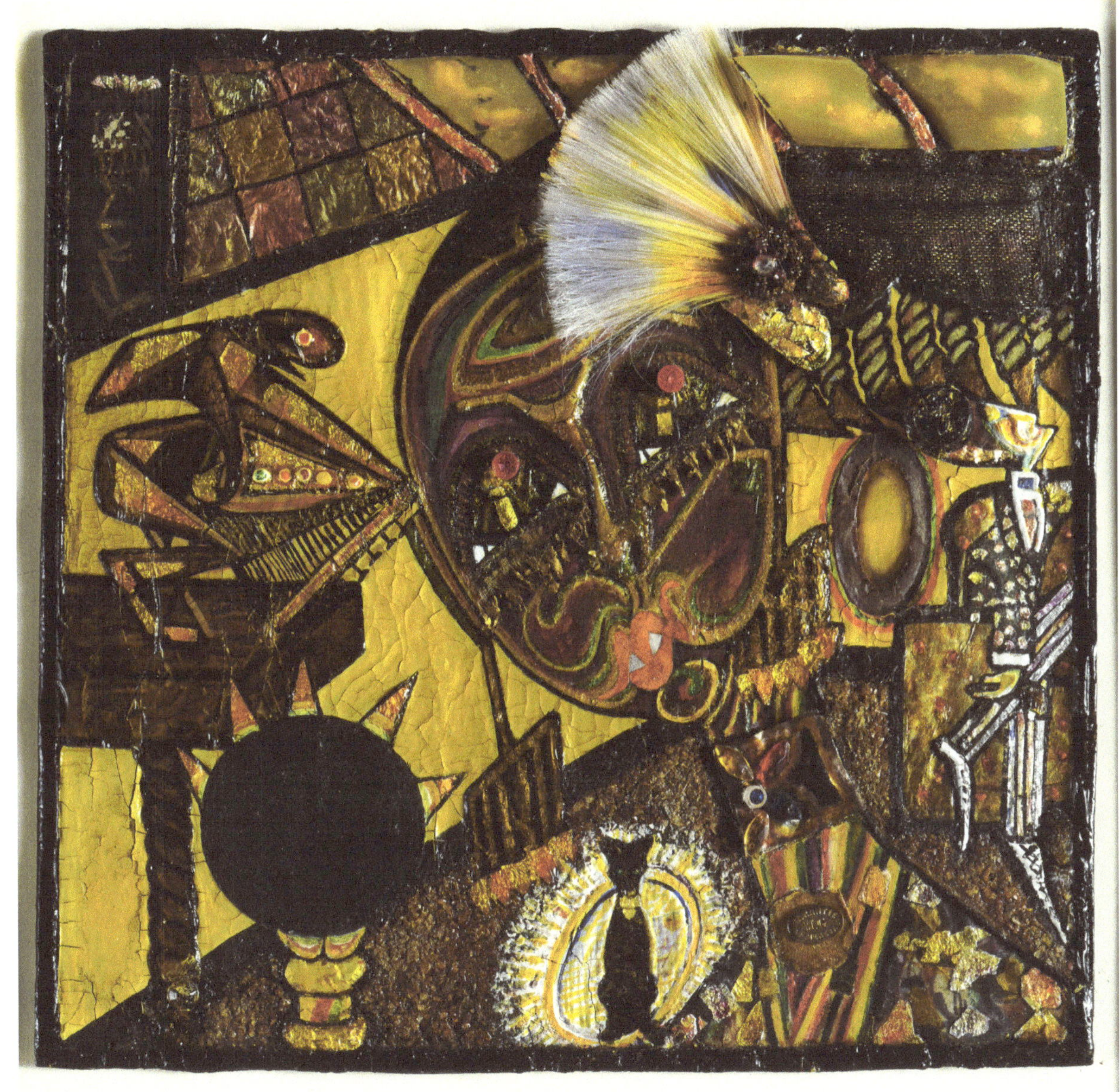

Filippo Tommaso Marinetti, 1876~1944

Filippo Marinetti was an Italian poet, writer, and playwright who founded and led the Futurism movement. His innovative ideas greatly influenced the arts and literature of the early 20th century.

Born in 1876 to a lawyer father and an art-loving mother, Marinetti spent his childhood in Alessandria before moving to France in 1884 to study philosophy, law, and literature.

On February 20, 1909, he gained international attention by publishing the Manifesto del Futurismo in the French newspaper Le Figaro. In this manifesto, he rejected tradition and proposed a new artistic vision centered around themes of machinery, speed, violence, and youth. He argued that Futurism should break away from past art and celebrate the dynamism and innovation of the modern world. Marinetti was also active as a playwright and poet, with notable works including La boîte à électrique and Les amoureux des bombes.

In addition to his artistic pursuits, Marinetti was passionate about political activities. He resonated deeply with Italian nationalism and fascism, supporting Benito Mussolini's fascist movement. He was one of the founding members of the Fascist Party in 1919 and held various political roles under Mussolini's government, believing that fascism, like Futurism, could break from the past and build a new future. During World War II, he continued to advocate for Futurism and fascism. However, after the war, his political stance and activities faced significant criticism, and he died of a heart attack in Bellagio on December 2, 1944.

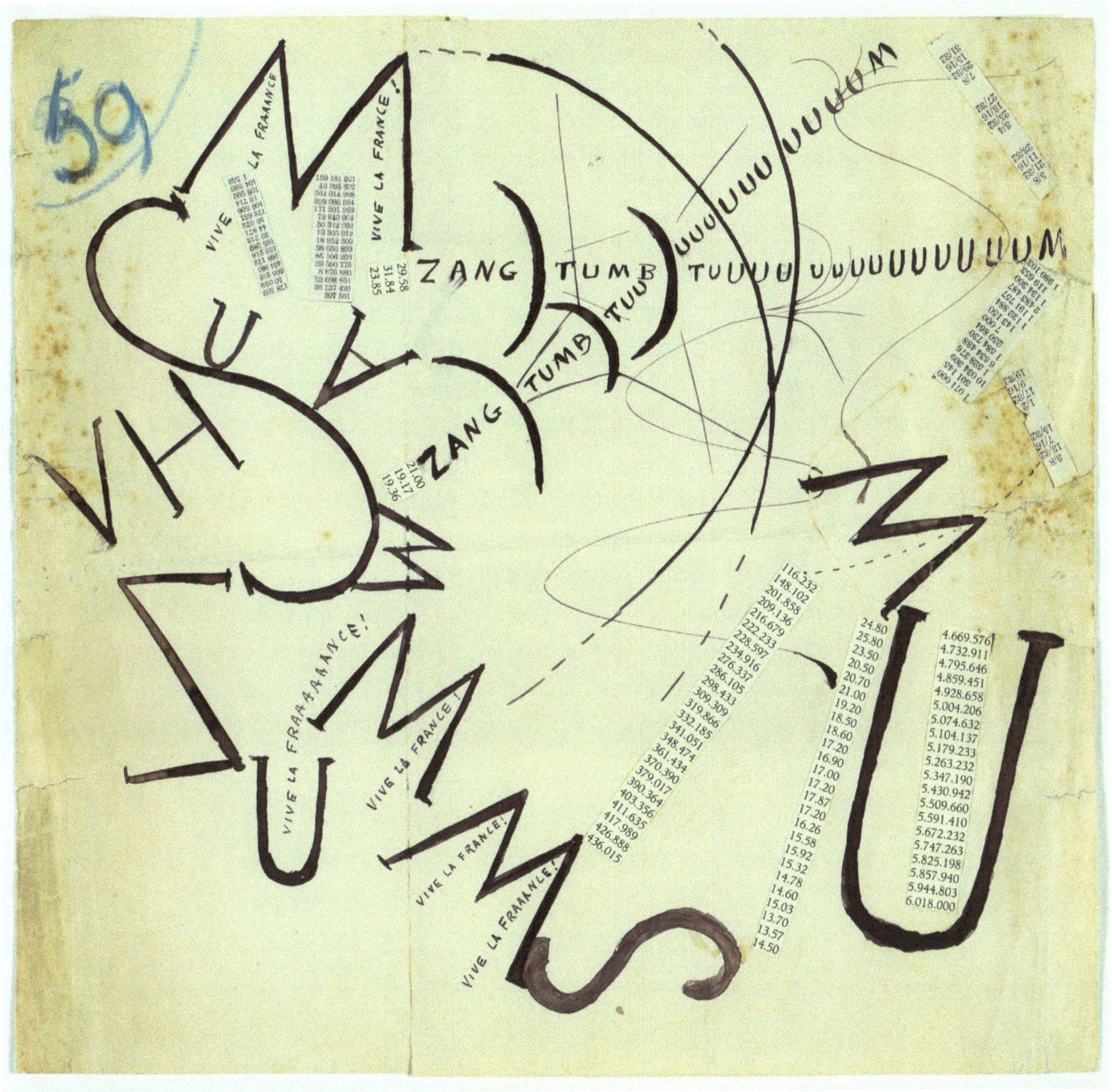
ZANG TUMB TUUUU UUUUUUUUUUM
ZANG TUMB TUUU
VIVE LA FRANCE!
VIVE LA FRAAANCE
VIVE LA FRAAAAANCE!

Francis Picabia, 1879~1953

Francis Picabia was a French painter and poet who created an original artistic world by navigating various movements, including Impressionism, Cubism, Dadaism, and Surrealism. Born and raised in Paris, he received formal art education at the École des Beaux-Arts and the National School of Decorative Arts. He began painting Impressionistic works, greatly inspired by the landscapes of Alfred Sisley.

In 1909, after becoming familiar with Impressionism, Picabia shifted his focus to Cubism. Inspired by the works of Marcel Duchamp, he co-founded the Section d'Or in 1912, a group that emphasized harmony and rhythm in geometric forms as a branch of Cubism. Picabia produced works that fused Cubism with his own unique style. He also exhibited his abstract works at the Armory Show in New York, receiving critical acclaim. Following this success, he returned to New York in 1915, contributing to the formation of the New York Dadaist Association alongside Duchamp and Man Ray. However, his interest in Dadaism was short-lived.

In 1917, Picabia focused on expressing human forms through mechanical imagery, gaining significant praise for his "original drawings inspired by machines." Four years later, he parted ways with Dadaism and joined the Surrealist movement. Actively using collage techniques, he sought to express three-dimensional space by layering transparent images without using perspective, creating a unique visual effect in his works. After World War II, Picabia returned to his hometown of Paris, where he resumed painting abstractions and writing poetry. He passed away in 1953 at the age of 74.

MOUVEMENT
DADA
ARENSBERG
GUILLAUME APOLLINAIRE
PICABIA
BRANCOUSY
KANDINSKY
PICASSO
BRAQUE
DELAUNAY
ARCHIPENKO
ERICK SATYE
VARÈSE
ALICE BAILLY
MARIE LAURENCIN
GLEIZES
METZINGER
DERAIN
MAX JACOB
MATISSE
MALLARME
SEURAT
VOLLARD
CEZANNE
RENOIR
RODIN
COROT
INGRES
RIB. DESSAIGNE
G. BUFFET
M. DUCHAMP
J. VILLON
TR. TZARA
H. ARP
DE ZAYAS
CROTTI
STIEGLITZ
JANCO
JULIETTE ROCHE
LEGER
"391"
PARIS - NEW-YORK
Francis Picabia 1919

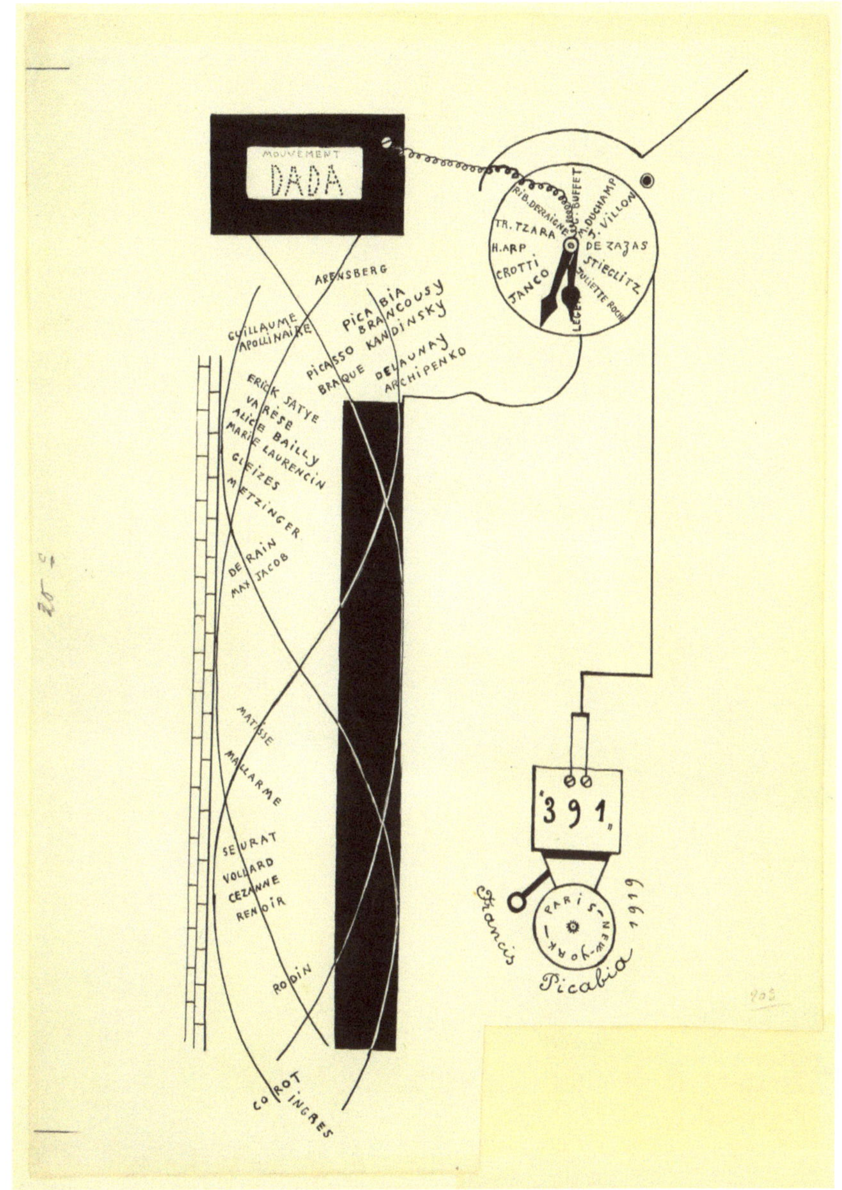

51.1 x 36.2 cm

New York, 1913

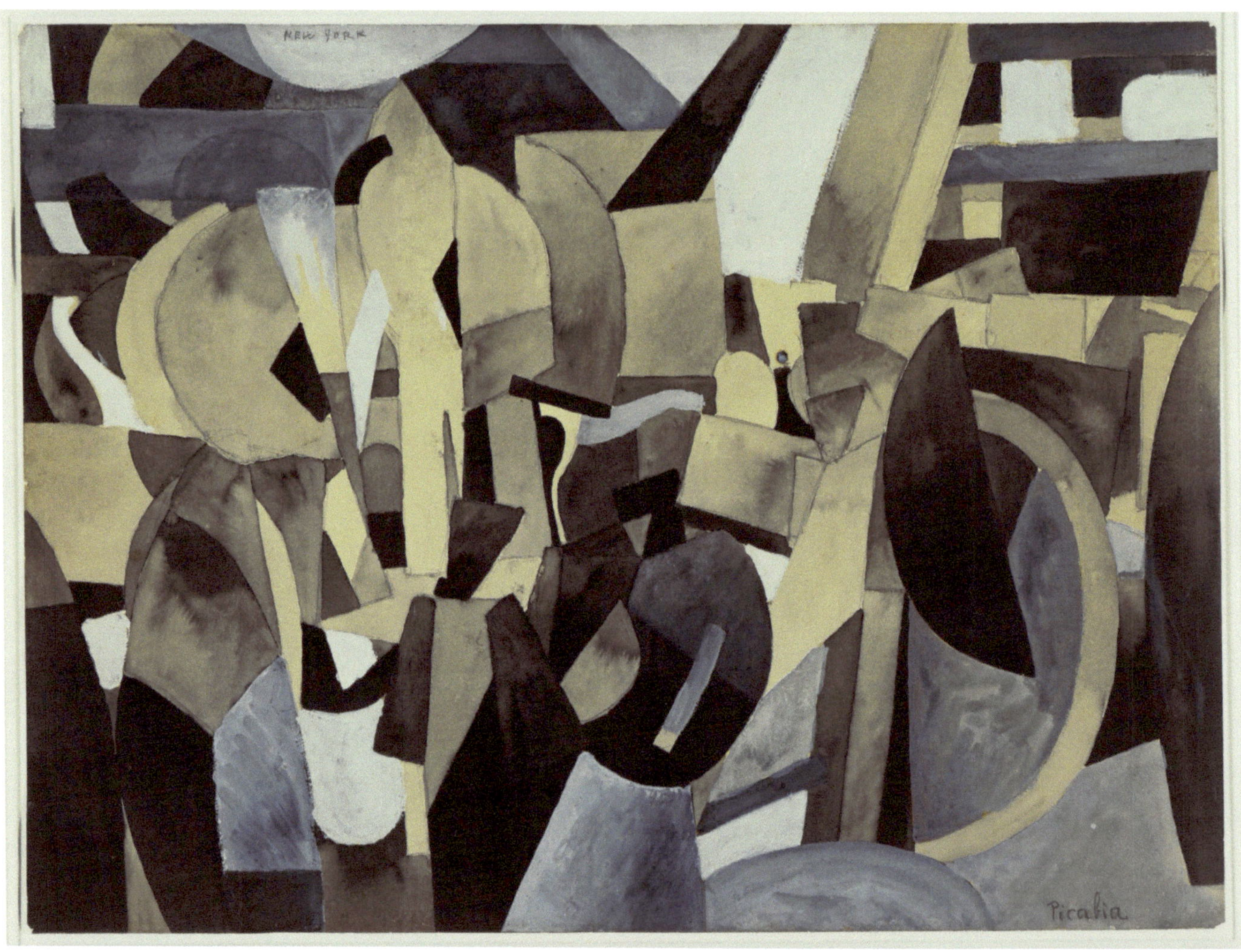

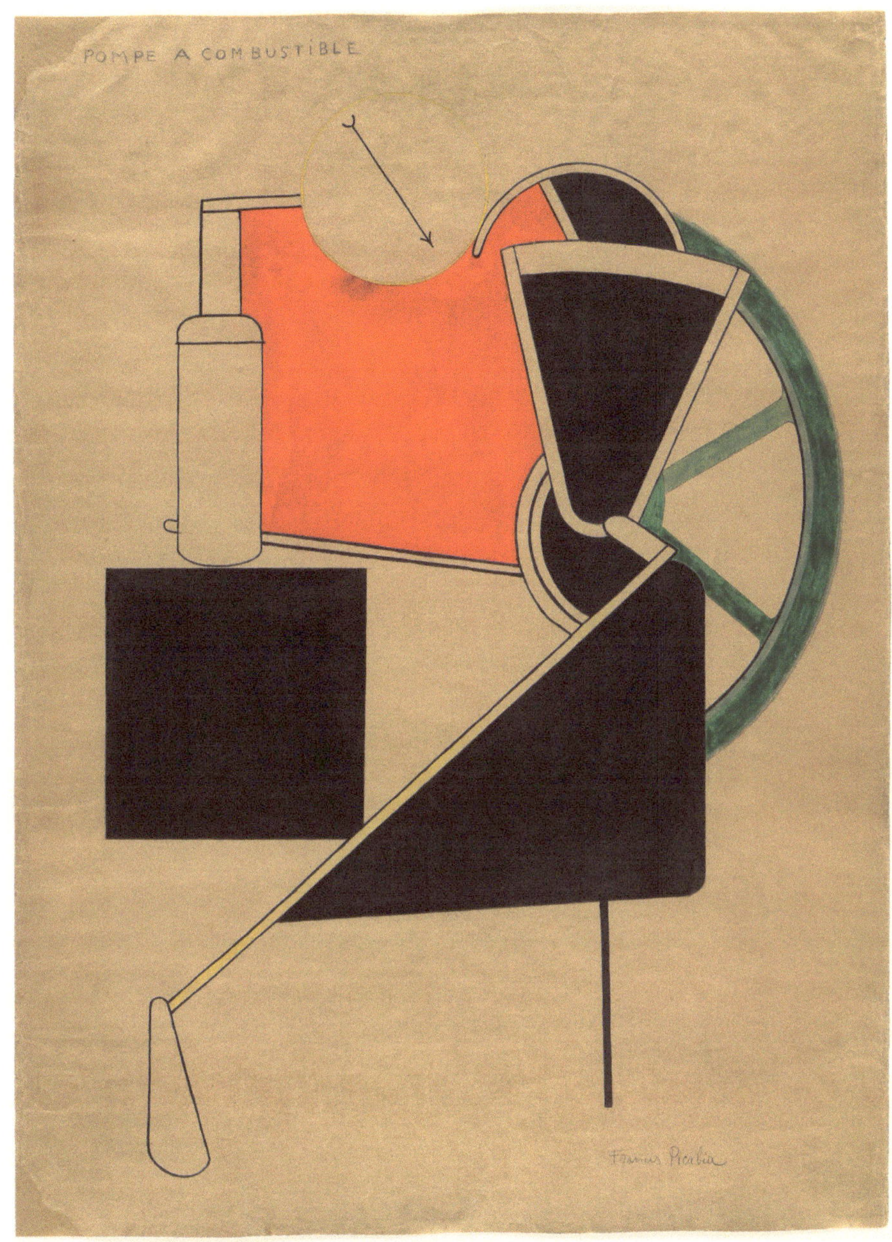
POMPE A COMBUSTIBLE
Francis Picabia

Henri Emile Benoit Matisse, 1869~1954

Henri Matisse, a renowned French painter celebrated for his work in various art forms including paper cutouts and graphic art, was born in Le Cateau-Cambrésis, France. As a teenager, while working as an assistant to a lawyer, he began taking drawing classes and became captivated by art during his recovery from appendicitis. Following his mother's advice, he enrolled in the École des Beaux-Arts in Paris, where he studied painting under the Symbolist artist Gustave Moreau.

Influenced by French Impressionism, Matisse created his own unique works characterized by an obsession with color and form. His pieces left a strong impression on viewers through their distinctive compositions and combinations of color. Matisse's early works featured dark tones, but after a summer vacation in Brittany, his art began to reflect vibrant colors and natural light. He later experimented with various painting styles and techniques of light, influenced by Fauvism. His collaboration with André Derain further enlivened and intensified his work. Alongside his success as a painter, he excelled in design, particularly known for his curtain and stained glass designs.

As a prominent artist representing France, Matisse maintained a consistent presence and gained international recognition. He was notably associated with a group of painters known as the "Fauves" and had a famous friendship with Pablo Picasso. Through his relationship with Sergei Shchukin, he introduced his works to Russia and received the French Legion of Honor. Diagnosed with duodenal cancer in 1940, he continued to paint even after surgery, turning to "cut-outs" with scissors, which led to the creation of a new art form.

Design for cover of Exhibition H. Matisse

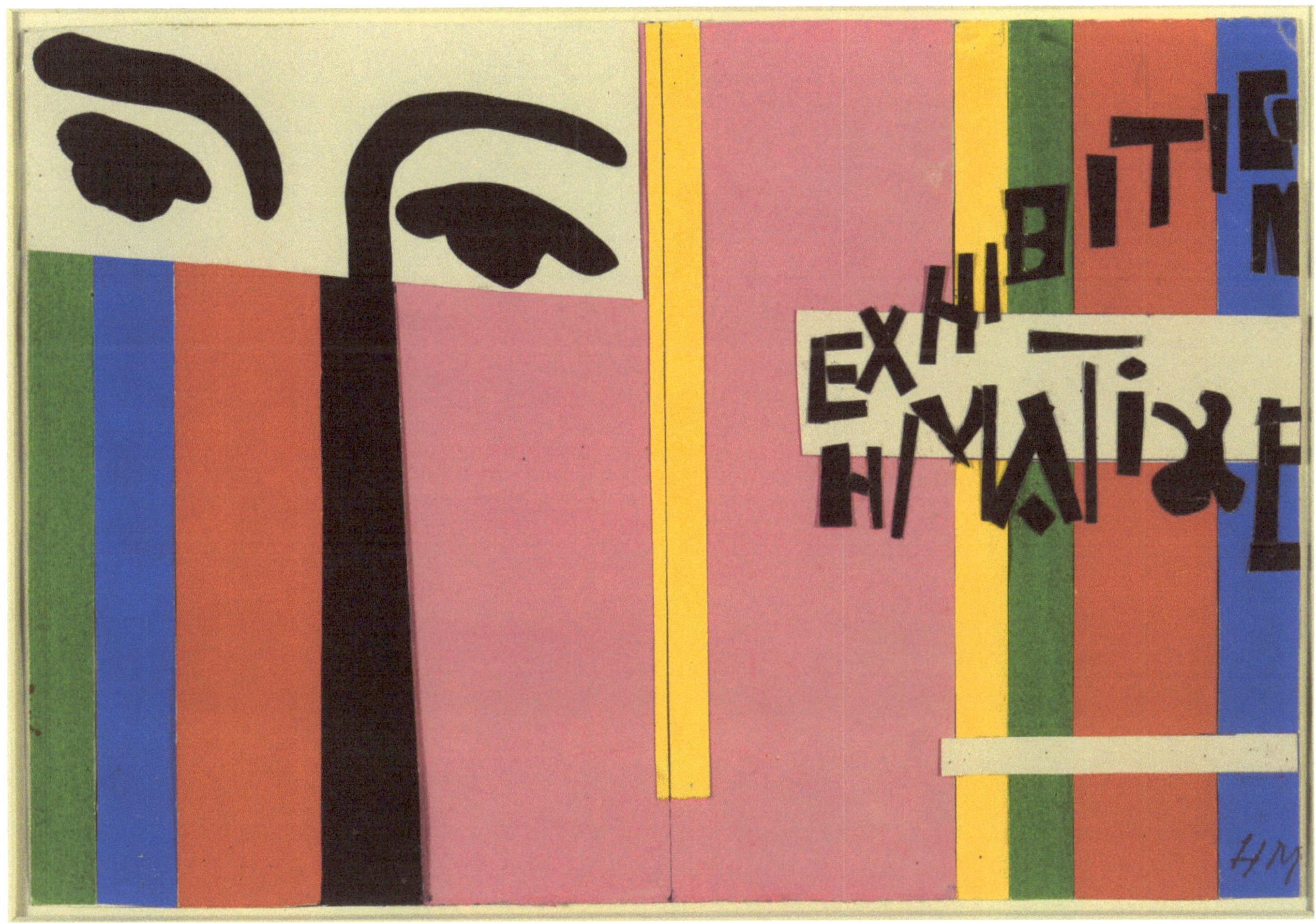

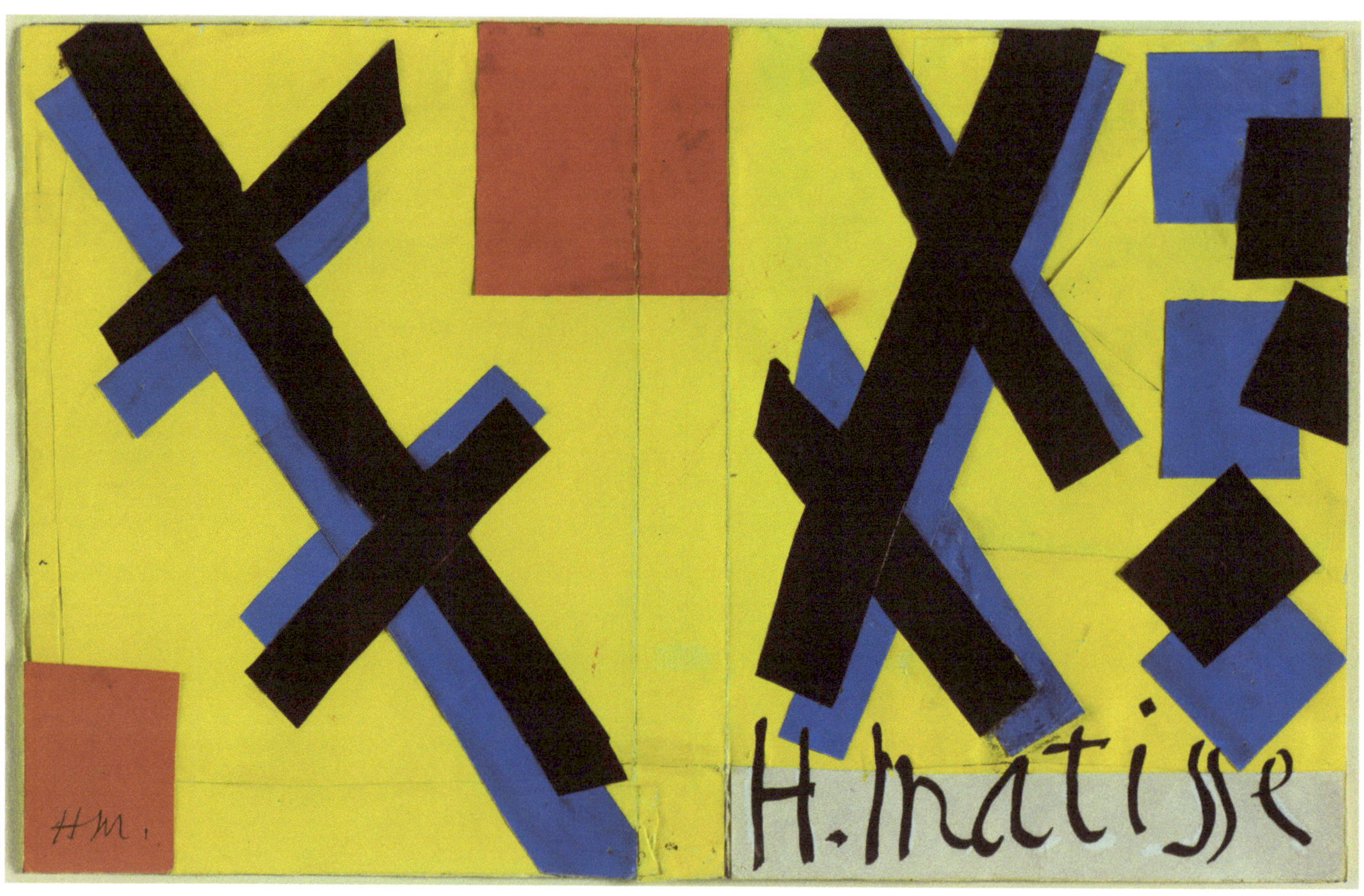

27 x 42.9 cm

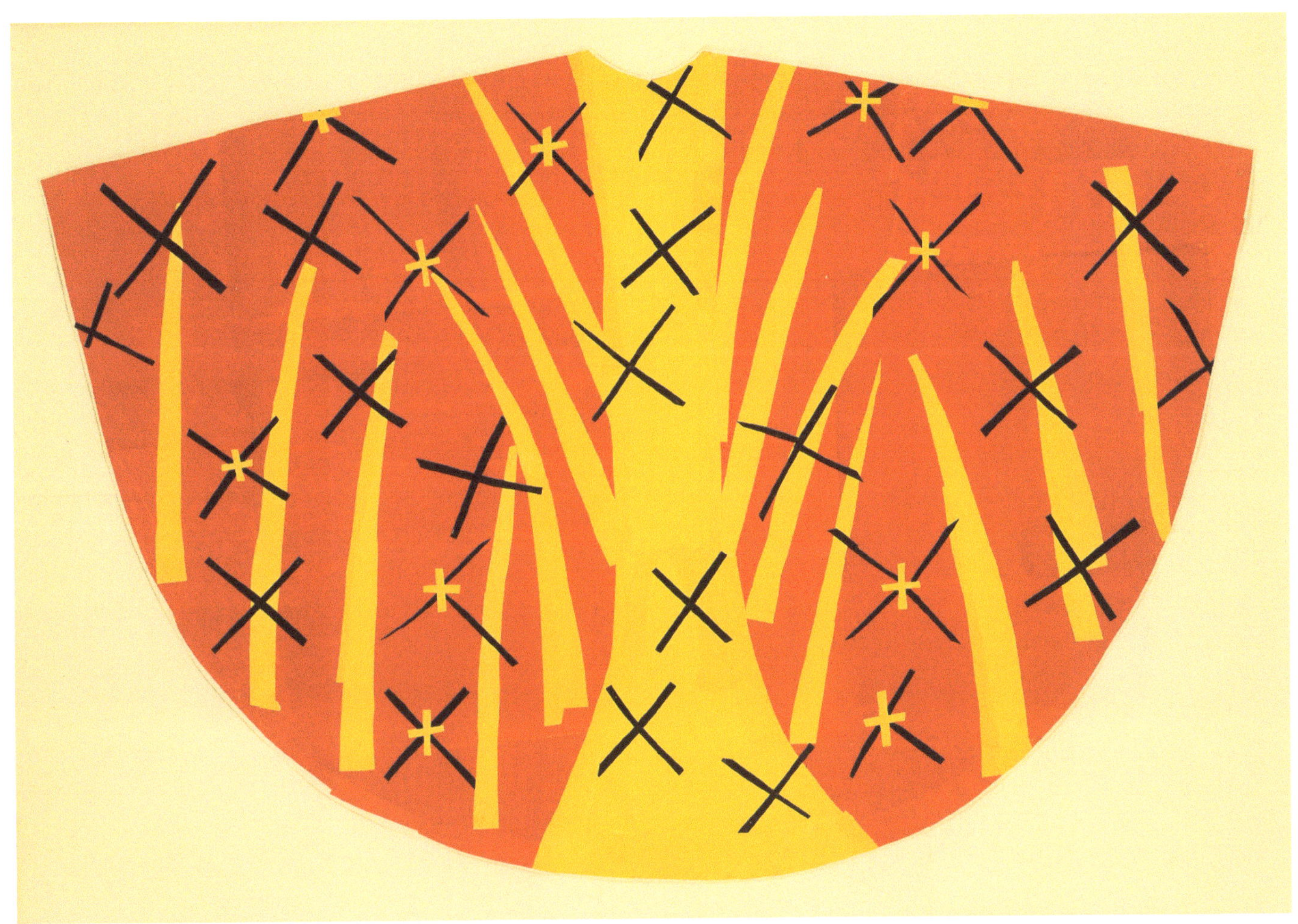

Joaquín Torres-García, 1874~1949

Joaquín Torres-García was born in 1874 in Montevideo, Uruguay. After studying art in Barcelona, Spain, he encountered avant-garde artists in the early 20th century, forming connections with renowned figures like Pablo Picasso. Torres-García worked across various media, creating murals and illustrations for newspapers and magazines, and collaborated with Antoni Gaudí on stained glass for the Palma de Mallorca Cathedral and the Sagrada Família in Barcelona.

In 1929, he moved to Paris, where he co-founded the first European abstract art group, "Cercle et Carré," with Piet Mondrian and Wassily Kandinsky, which later became known as Universal Constructivism. During this period, Torres-García began exploring a unique geometric abstract style that combined Constructivism and Cubism.

His works are characterized by a grid structure featuring ochre tones and a distinctive arrangement of symbolic elements. Upon returning to Uruguay, he established a Constructivist art association and announced his ideas to the world through the manifesto "The School of the South." His goal was to express authenticity through simplified structures and colors, free from formal decoration. He dedicated himself to teaching students and spreading modernist ideas.

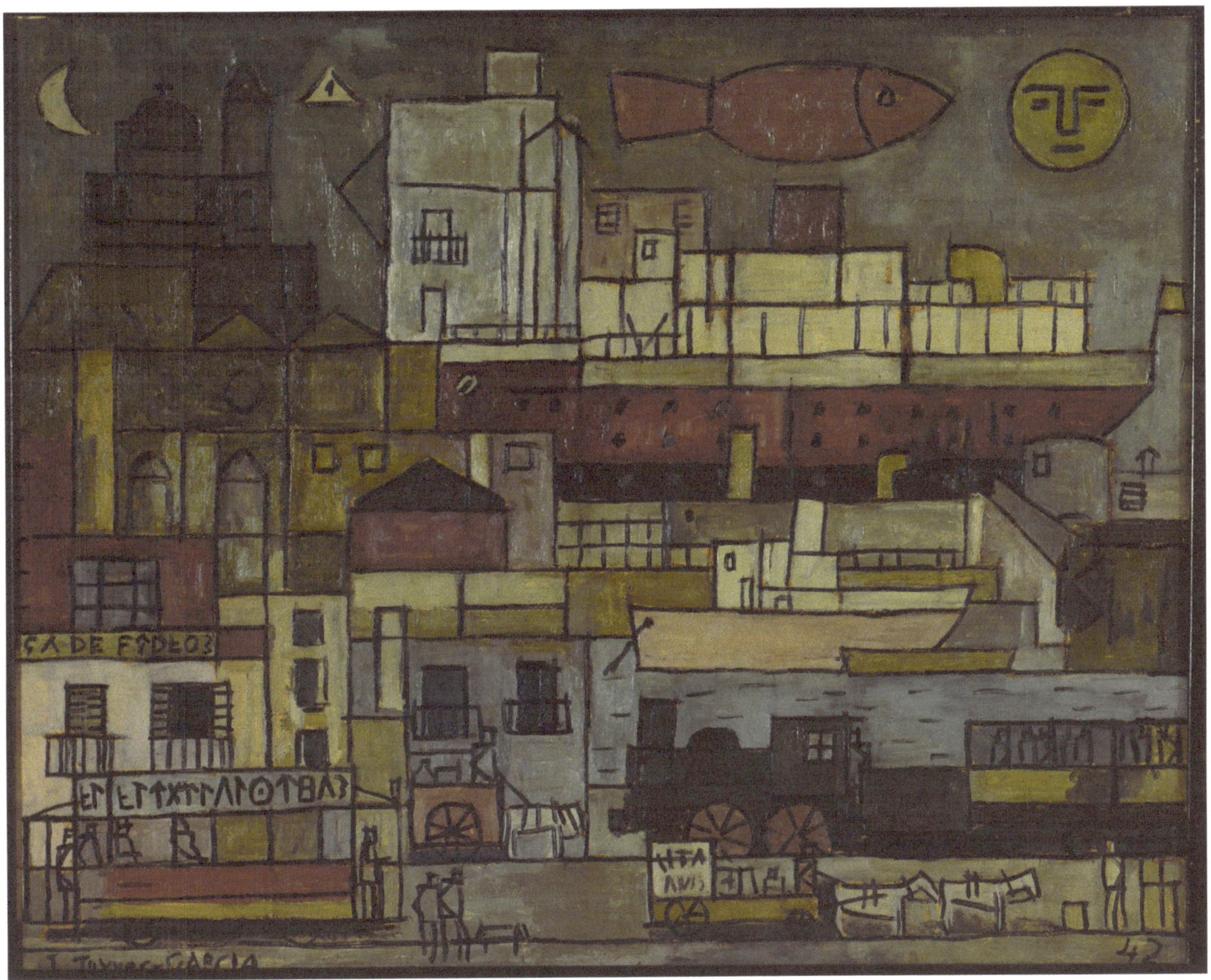

Lyubov Sergeyevna Popova, 1889~1924

Lyubov Sergeyevna Popova was born on April 24, 1889, in Ivanovskoe, near Moscow, Russia. Growing up in a wealthy upper-class family, she was exposed to art and culture from a young age and began receiving private art lessons from a tutor at the age of 11. She studied at the Moscow School of Painting, Sculpture and Architecture from 1906 to 1907, and then continued her art education at Konstantin Yuon's school from 1908 to 1909, where she developed a strong interest in both traditional Russian and European art.

In 1910, Popova traveled to Italy to study Renaissance art, where she was deeply impressed by the works she encountered, allowing her artistic vision to flourish. Two years later, she moved to Paris, where she formed friendships with Cubist painters such as Henri Le Fauconnier and Jean Metzinger. She was also influenced by Italian Futurist Umberto Boccioni, whose "Technical Manifesto of Futurist Sculpture" provided her with significant inspiration.

Upon returning to Moscow in 1913, Popova became an active participant in the Russian avant-garde movement. From 1914 to 1916, she developed a keen interest in Russian Cubo-Futurism and collaborated with artists like Aleksandra Ekster, Nadezhda Udaltsova, and Olga Rozanova, participating in exhibitions such as "V Tramway V" and "0.10." The "V Tramway V" exhibition was a showcase for the Cubo-Futurism movement, while "0.10" marked the beginning of the Suprematist movement, centered around Kazimir Malevich, and introduced new directions in modern art. These exhibitions had a profound impact on the development of Russian avant-garde art and modern artistic progress.

In 1916, Popova joined Malevich's Suprematist group, which explored the essence of art through pure geometric forms and colors. She developed her own distinctive painting style known as "painterly architectonics," characterized by a blend of Western painting techniques, vibrant colors, and dynamic spatial compositions that conveyed both energy and softness. While influenced by Malevich, her focus remained primarily on the painterly aspect.

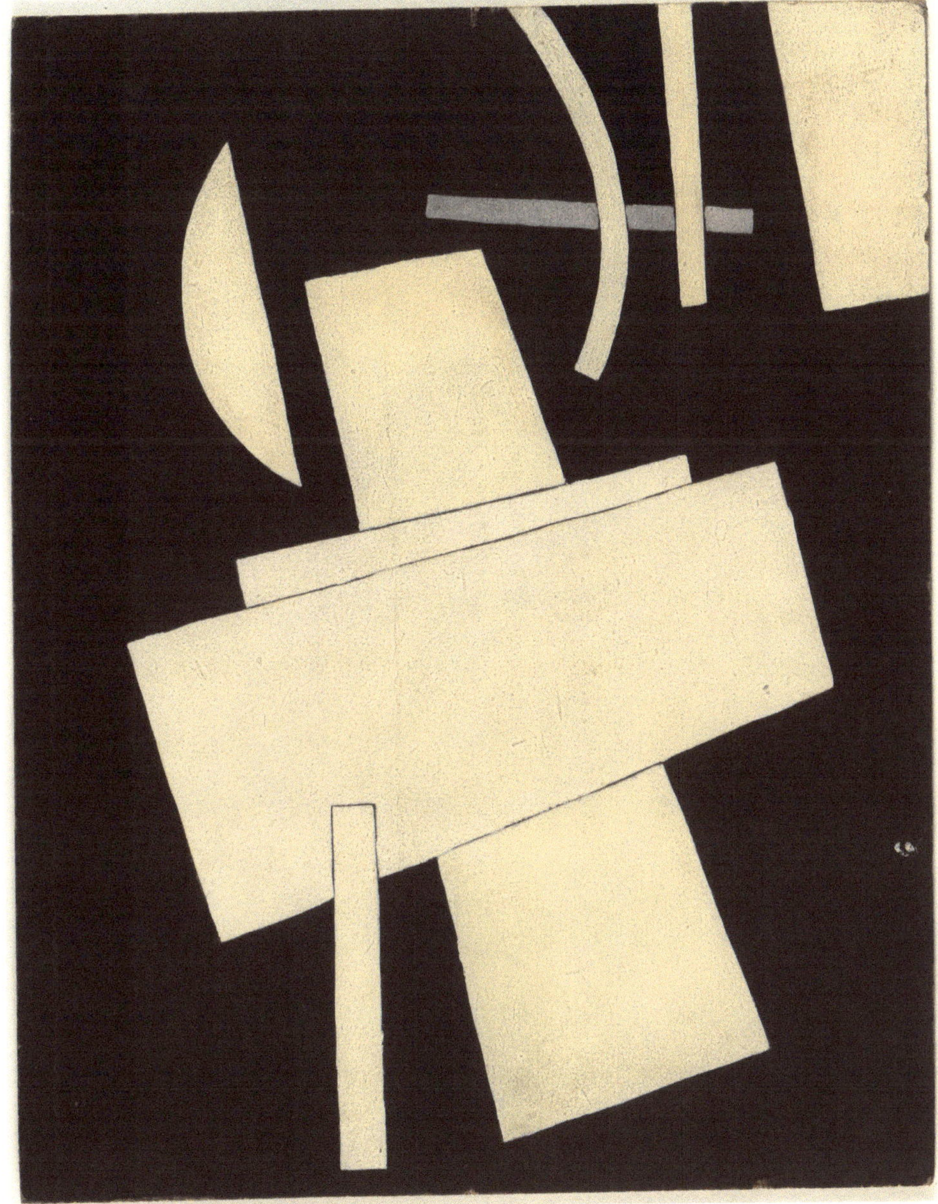

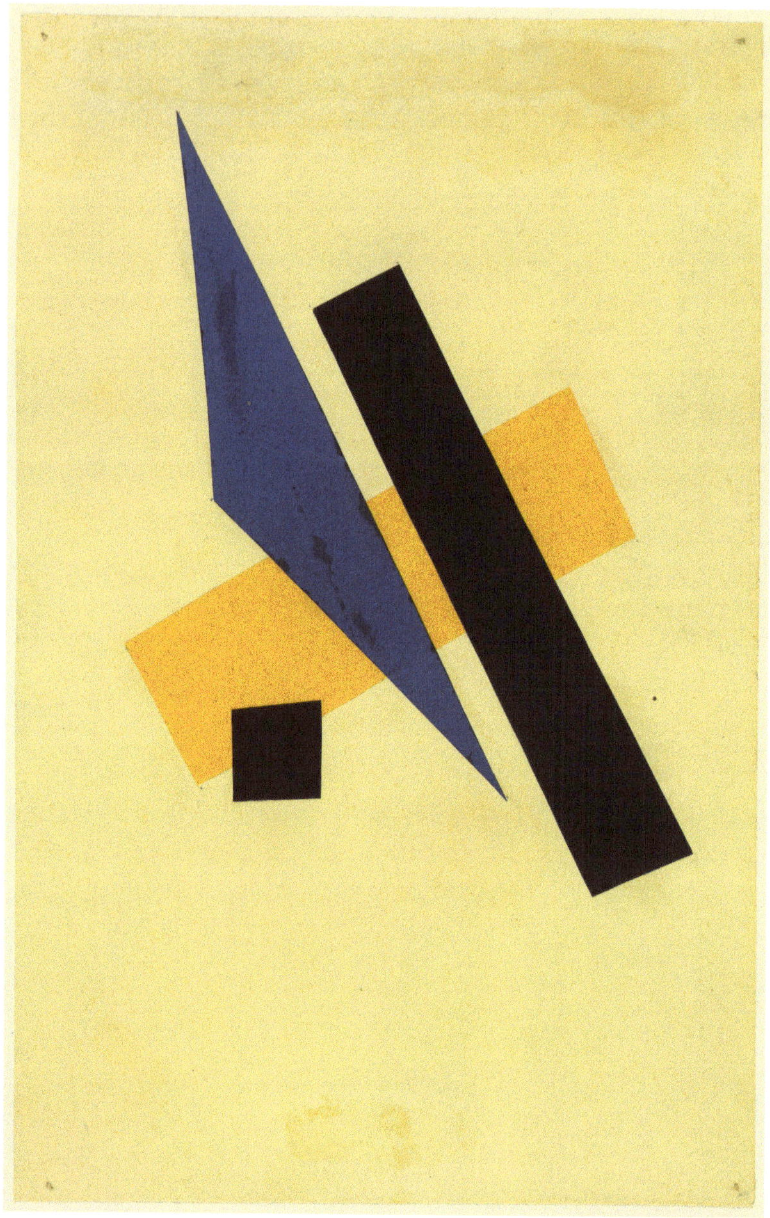

Maurice Denis, 1870~1943

Maurice Denis is known as a significant member of the French Post-Impressionist group, the Nabis. He worked as a painter, critic, and art theorist, engaging in a variety of roles within the art world.

Born in 1870 in Granville, France, Denis began studying at the École des Beaux-Arts in Paris at the age of 18. There, he met artists such as Émile Bernard and Paul Signac, which exposed him to Impressionism.

In the late 1890s, influenced by Paul Cézanne and Paul Gauguin, Denis joined the Nabis group and became a central figure within it. He primarily focused on themes of faith, love, and nature, emphasizing composition and color in his work. He referred to his artistic philosophy as "art pur," defining the role of the artist as one who expresses the beauty of the world and inspires others. Through his critical writings, he had a significant impact on the French art scene.

From 1893 to 1894, Denis spent a year in Pont-Aven with Cézanne and Gauguin, during which he sought to develop his unique style. His works, characterized by simple outlines and concise color areas, showcased a vibrant quality, viewing nature not merely as a subject but as a means to express a two-dimensional plane. In his later works, he increasingly emphasized religious themes.

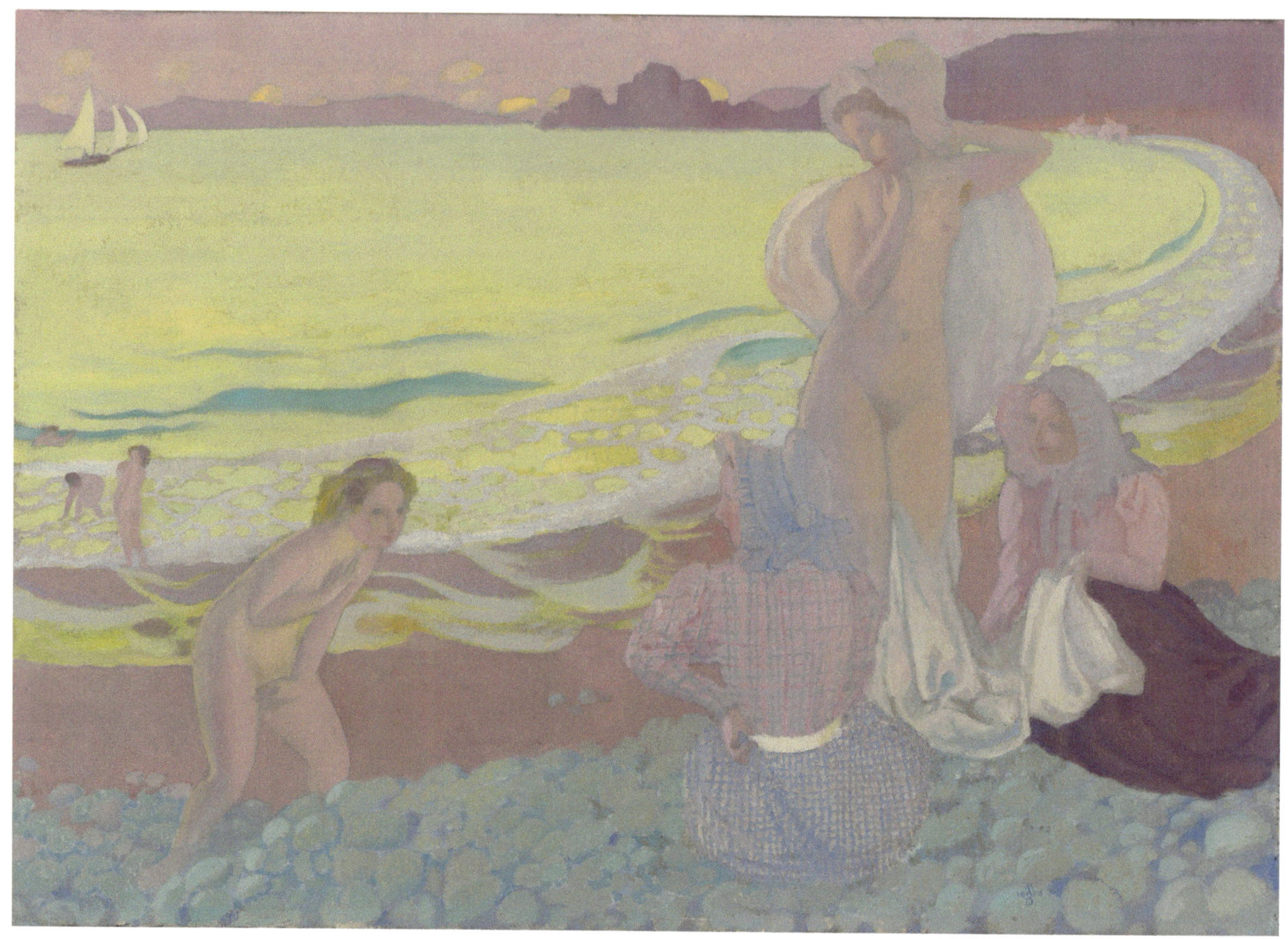

70 x 99 cm

Museum of Modern Art, New York, USA

Nikolai Suetin, 1897~1954

Nikolai Suetin was a prominent Russian painter and ceramicist, a key figure in the avant-garde art movement, known primarily for his contributions to Constructivism and Suprematism.

He was born on October 20, 1897, in Mikhaylovskoye, a village near Nizhny Novgorod, Russia. At the age of 20, he enrolled in an art school in Petrograd (now St. Petersburg), where he interacted with avant-garde artists and laid the foundation for his career, becoming involved in the Suprematist movement influenced by Kazimir Malevich. He created works in a style similar to Malevich's famous Suprematist pieces, developing abstract and geometric forms.

In the 1930s, Suetin became interested in ceramics and industrial design, showcasing his artistic talent at a state porcelain factory in Leningrad (now St. Petersburg). He applied Suprematist designs to ceramics, producing innovative works that are regarded as significant examples of Russian avant-garde design.

In the late 1940s and early 1950s, Suetin taught students at the Leningrad Academy of Arts, contributing to the education of future artists. He played a vital role in disseminating Suprematism and Constructivism through various media.

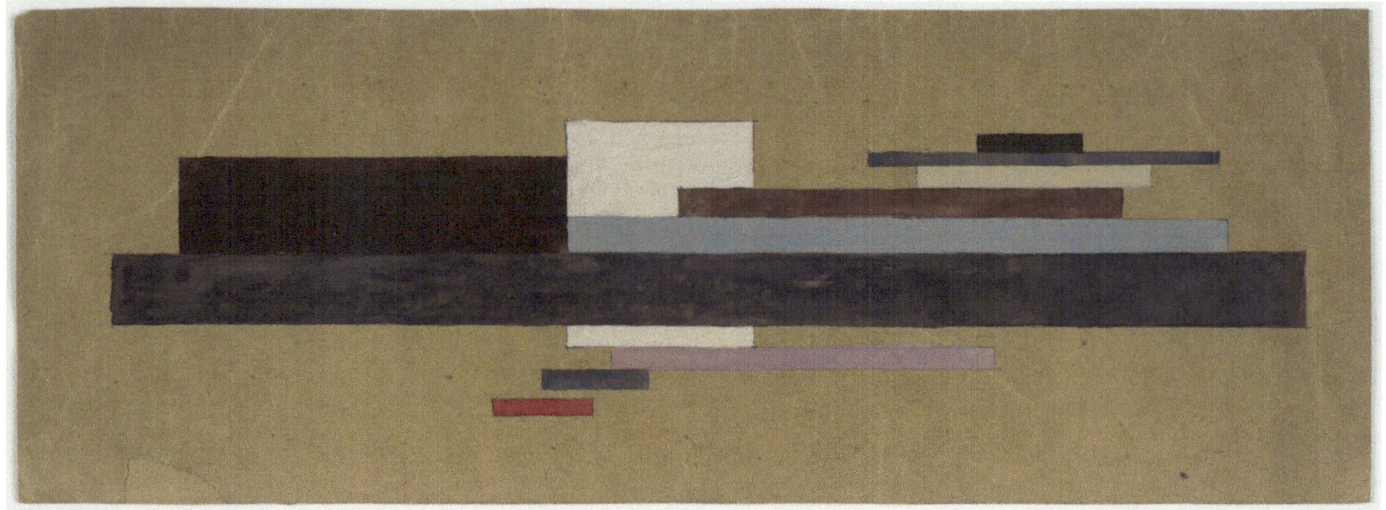

10.6 x 30.5 cm

Odilon Redon, 1840~1916

Odilon Redon was born in Bordeaux, France. His father amassed wealth through the slave trade in Louisiana, while his mother was of French Creole descent. Spending much of his childhood on an island, he grew up in an isolated environment that stimulated his imagination. Due to health issues, he spent a lot of time alone, exploring his inner world and dreams.

Redon is known for his symbolist works that embody unique beauty, particularly famous for his black paintings. His experiences as a soldier during the Franco-Prussian War (1870-71) influenced his art, allowing him to reflect the horrors and brutality of war in his work. After moving to Paris, he created numerous pieces and prints utilizing the color black.

In the 1890s, he produced more vibrant and fantastical works using color and pastels, showcasing mythological figures and Eastern elements in a variety of themes. His art is noted for its religious and mythological subjects, along with surrealistic elements, marking significant artistic progress.

Apparition in the Window, c.1892

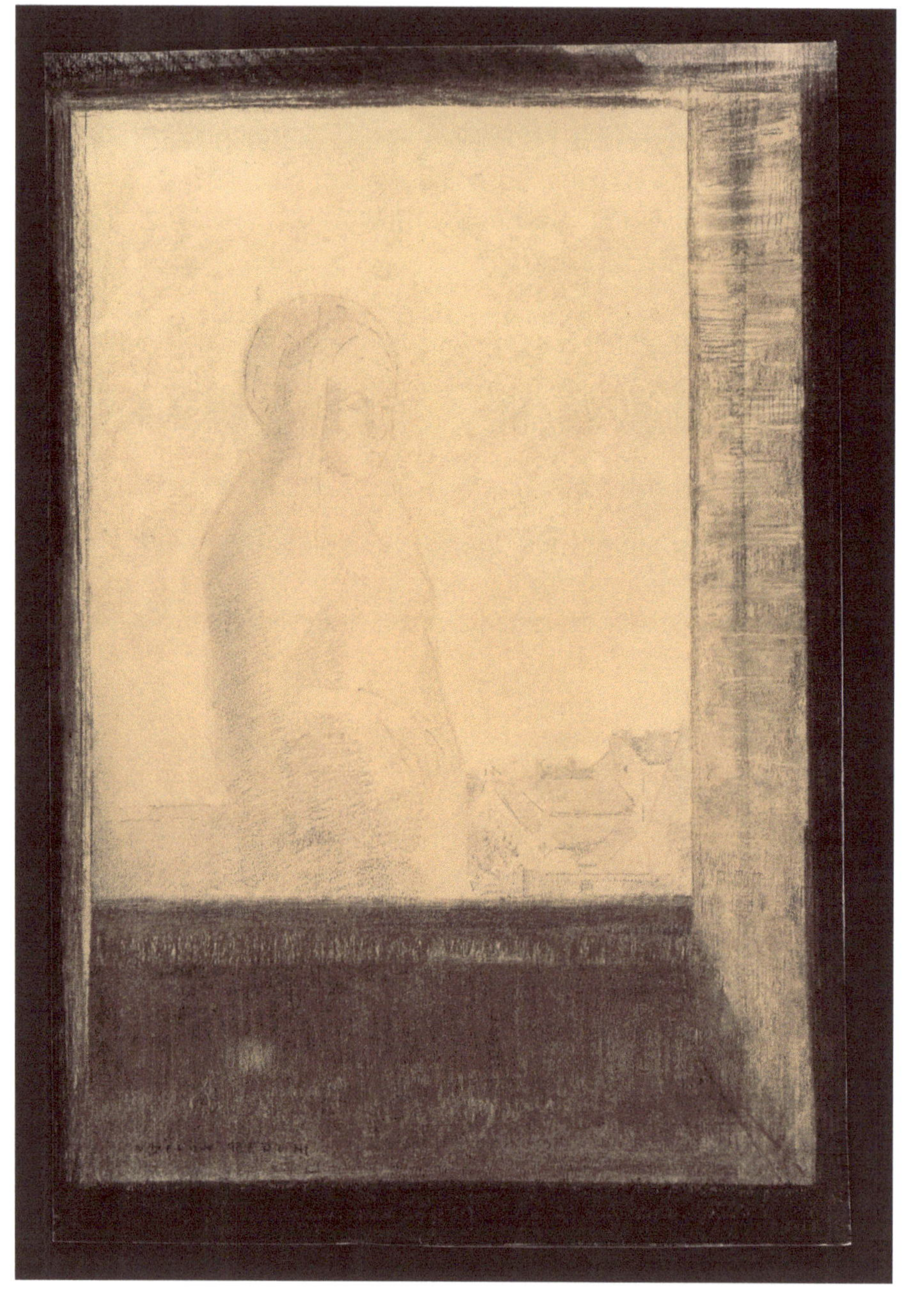

46 x 31.4 cm

Centaur Aiming at the Clouds, 1895

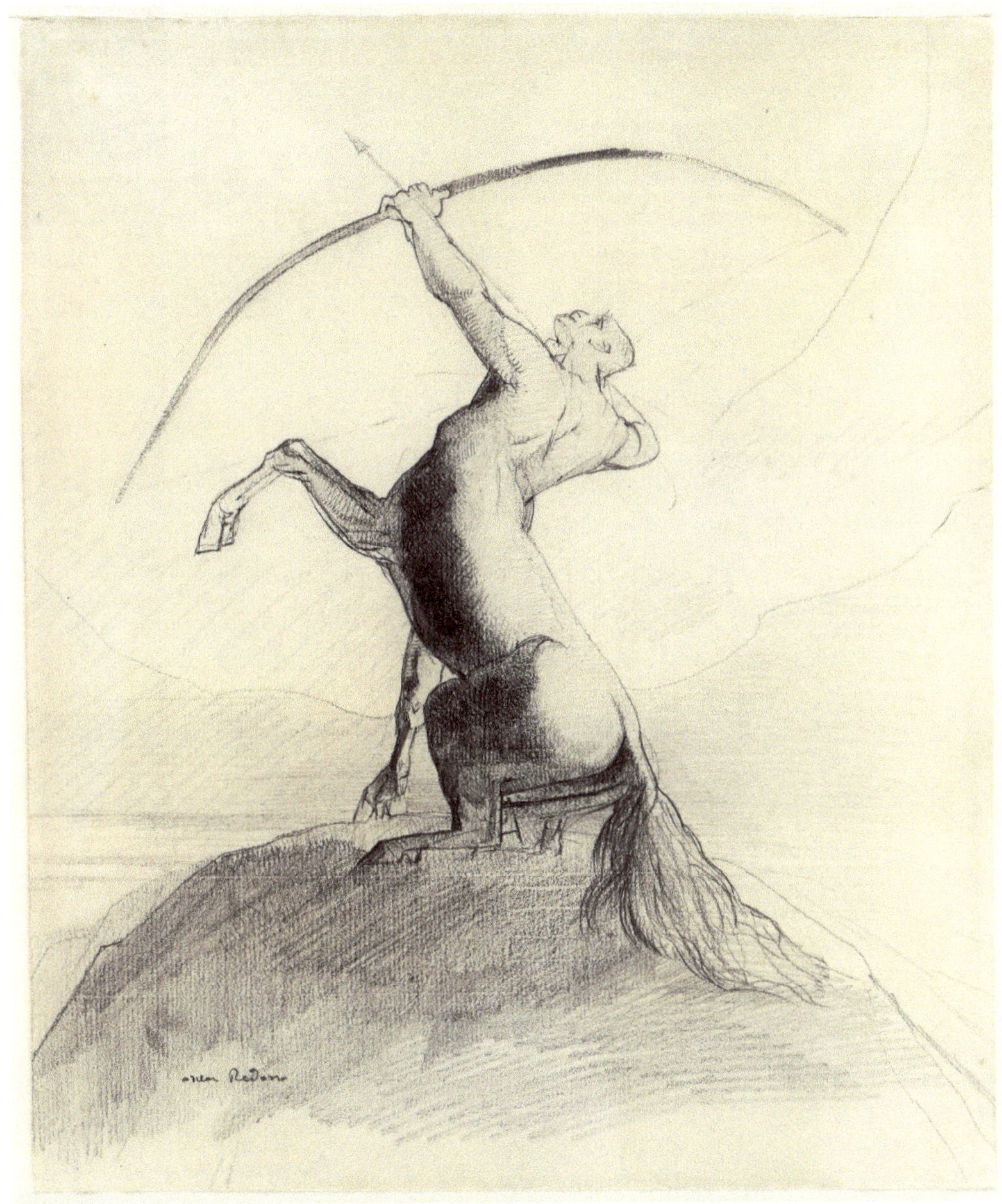

31.6 x 24.7 cm

National Gallery of Art, Washington D.C., USA

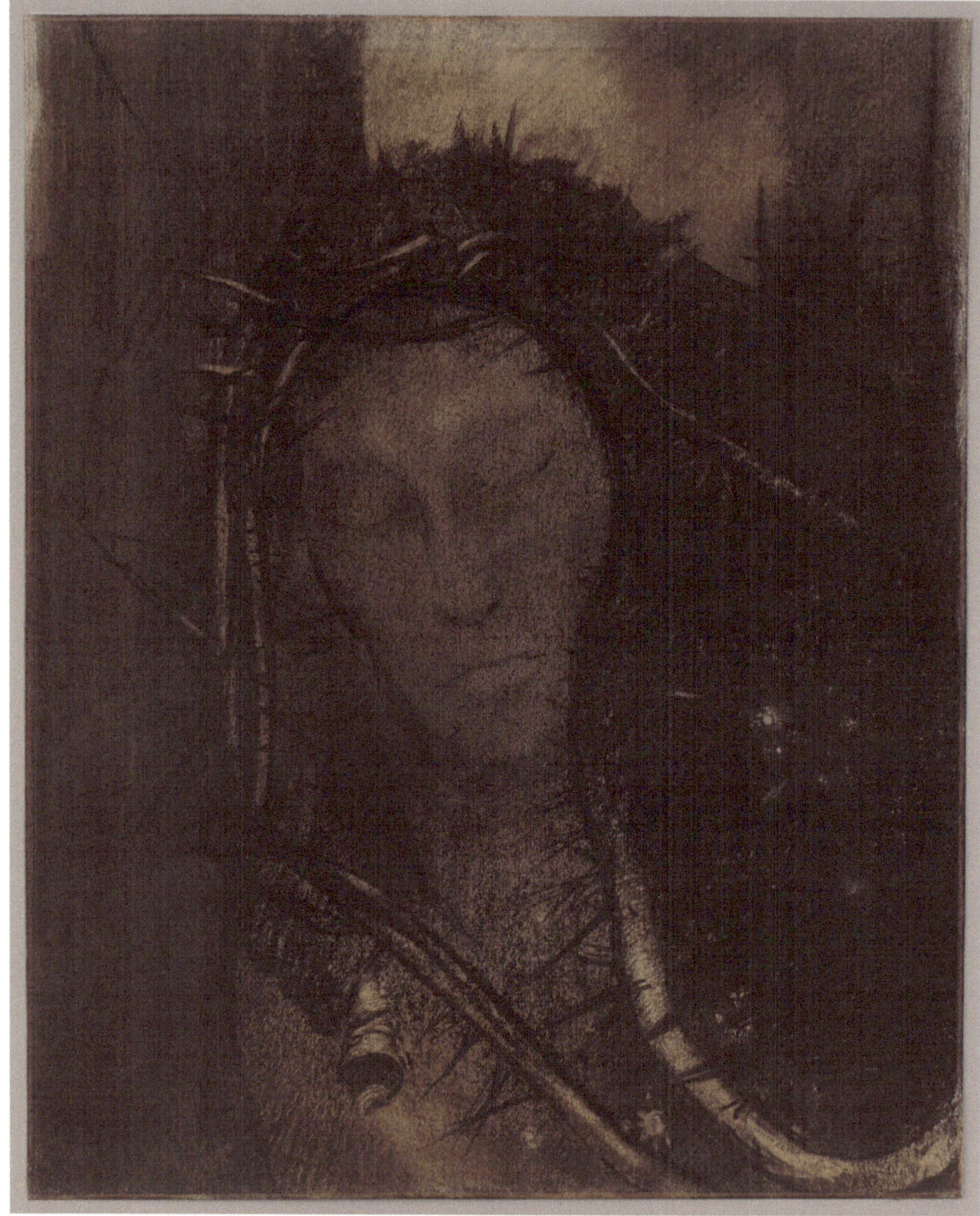

Diana, c.1900

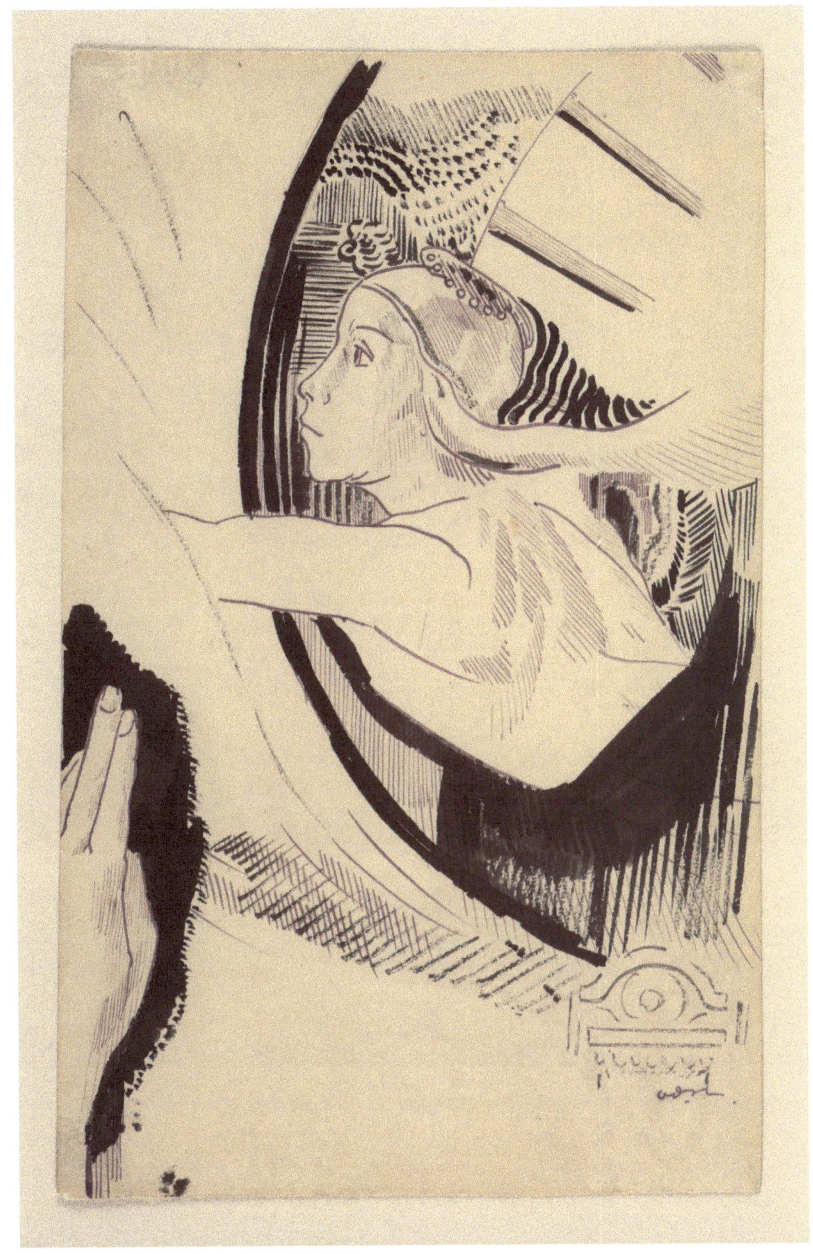

22.2 x 14.3 cm

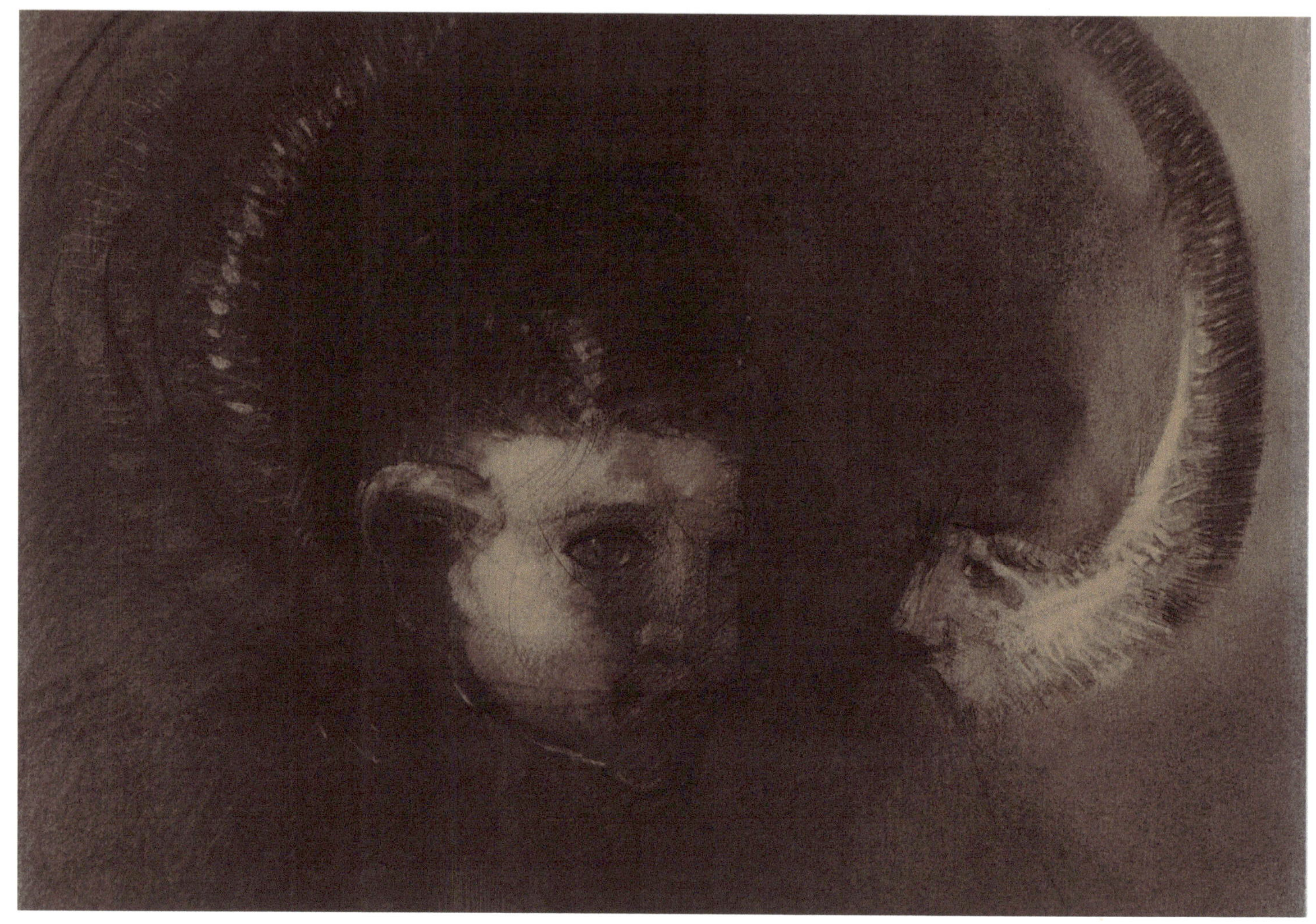

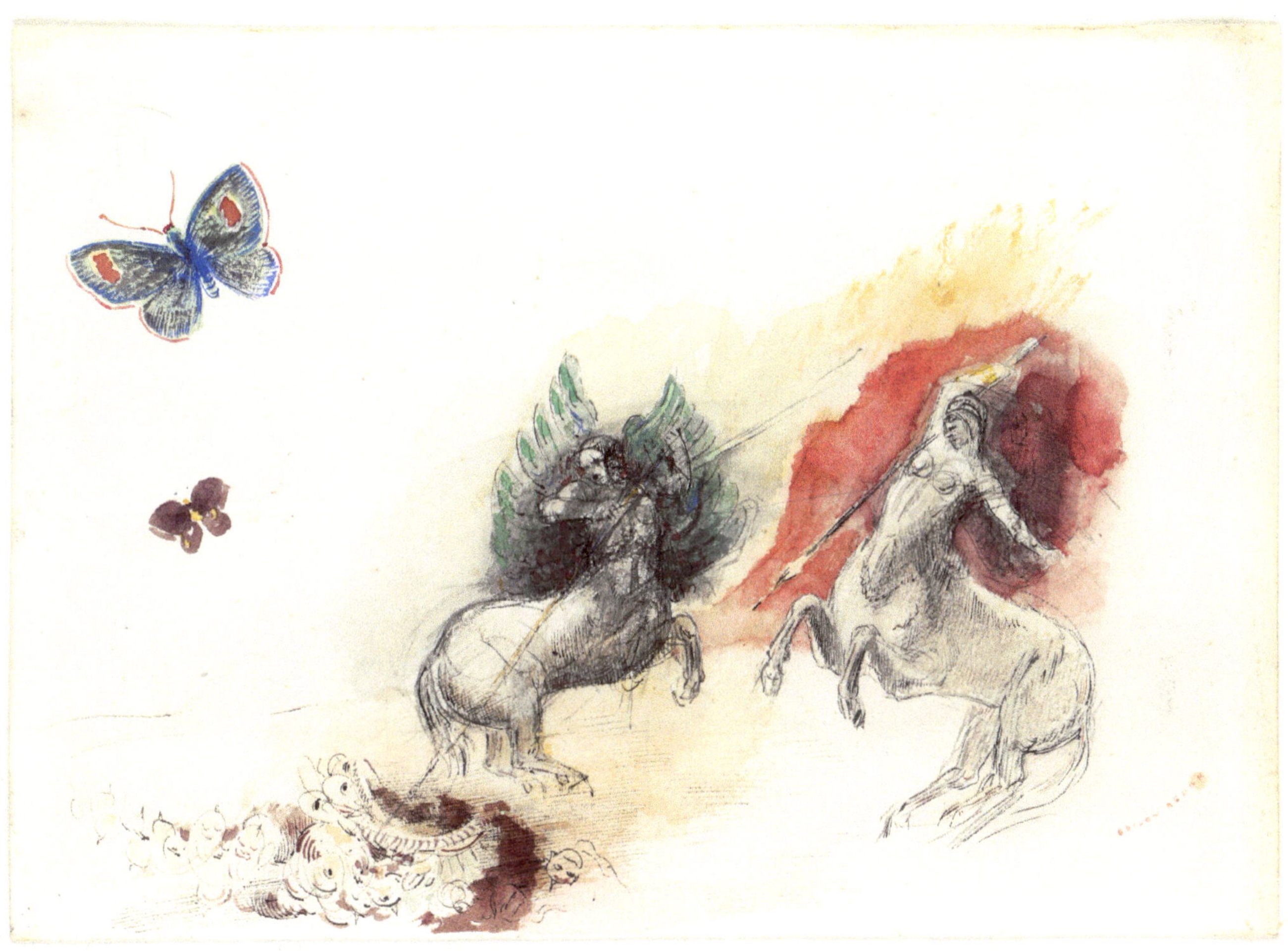

17.8 x 25.3 cm

Private Collection

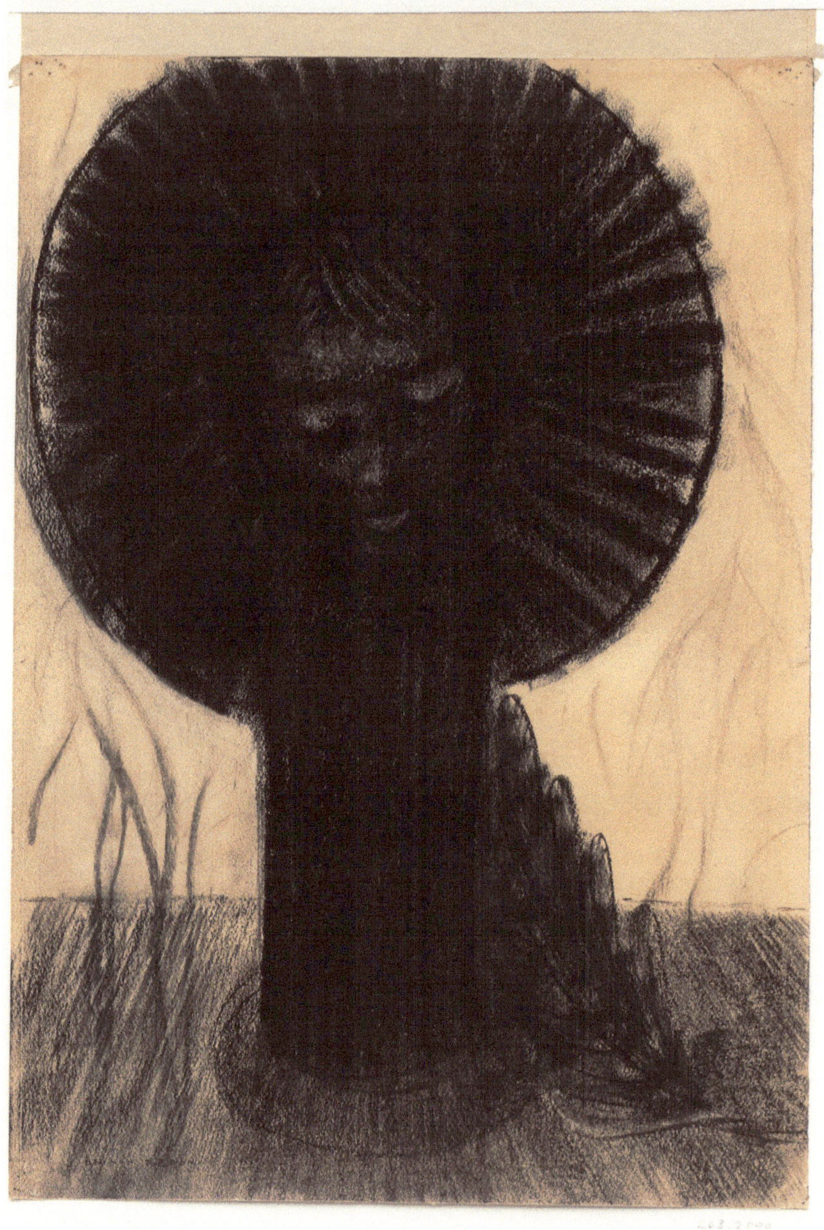

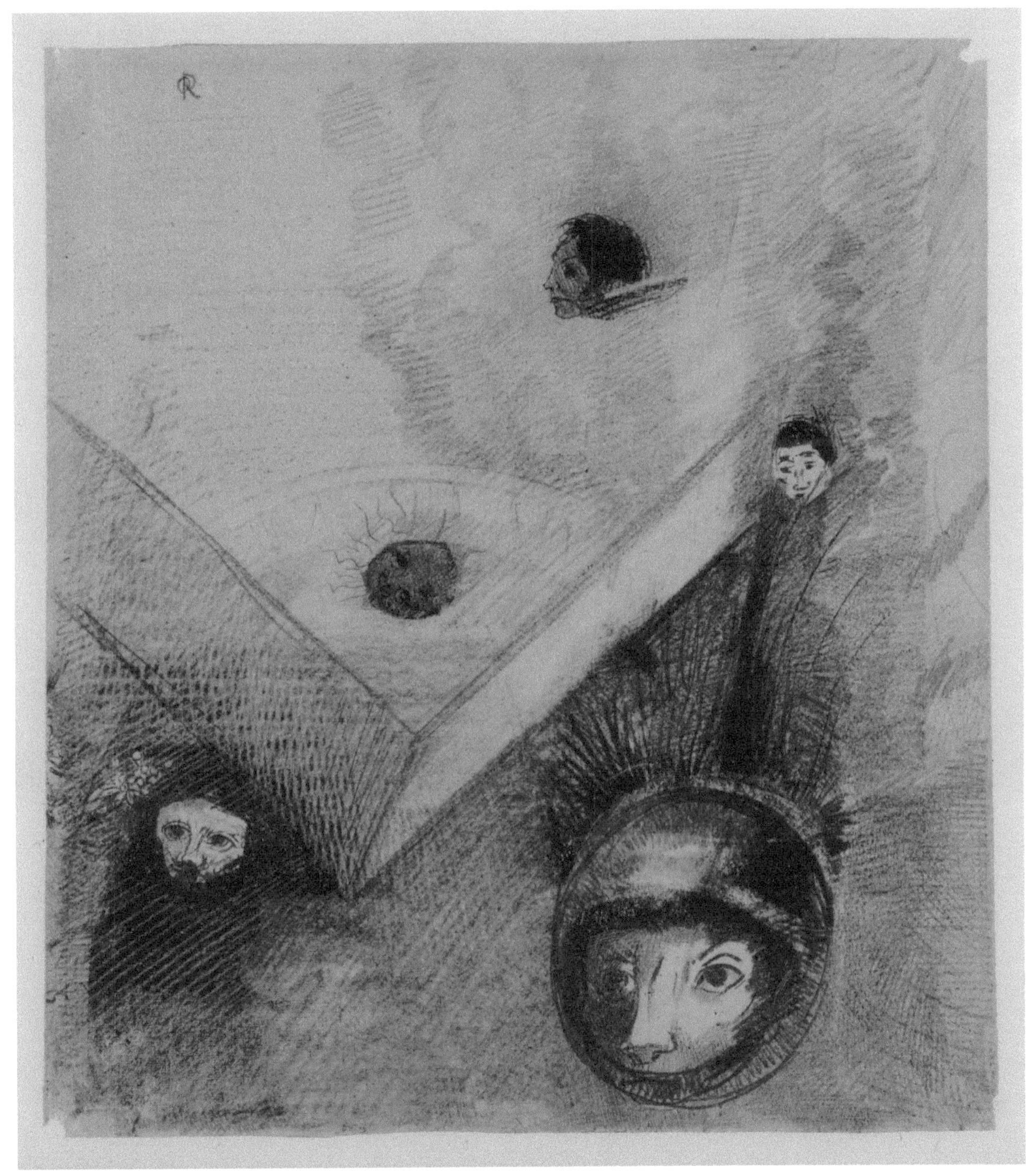

21.5 x 19.1 cm

National Gallery of Art, Washington D.C., USA

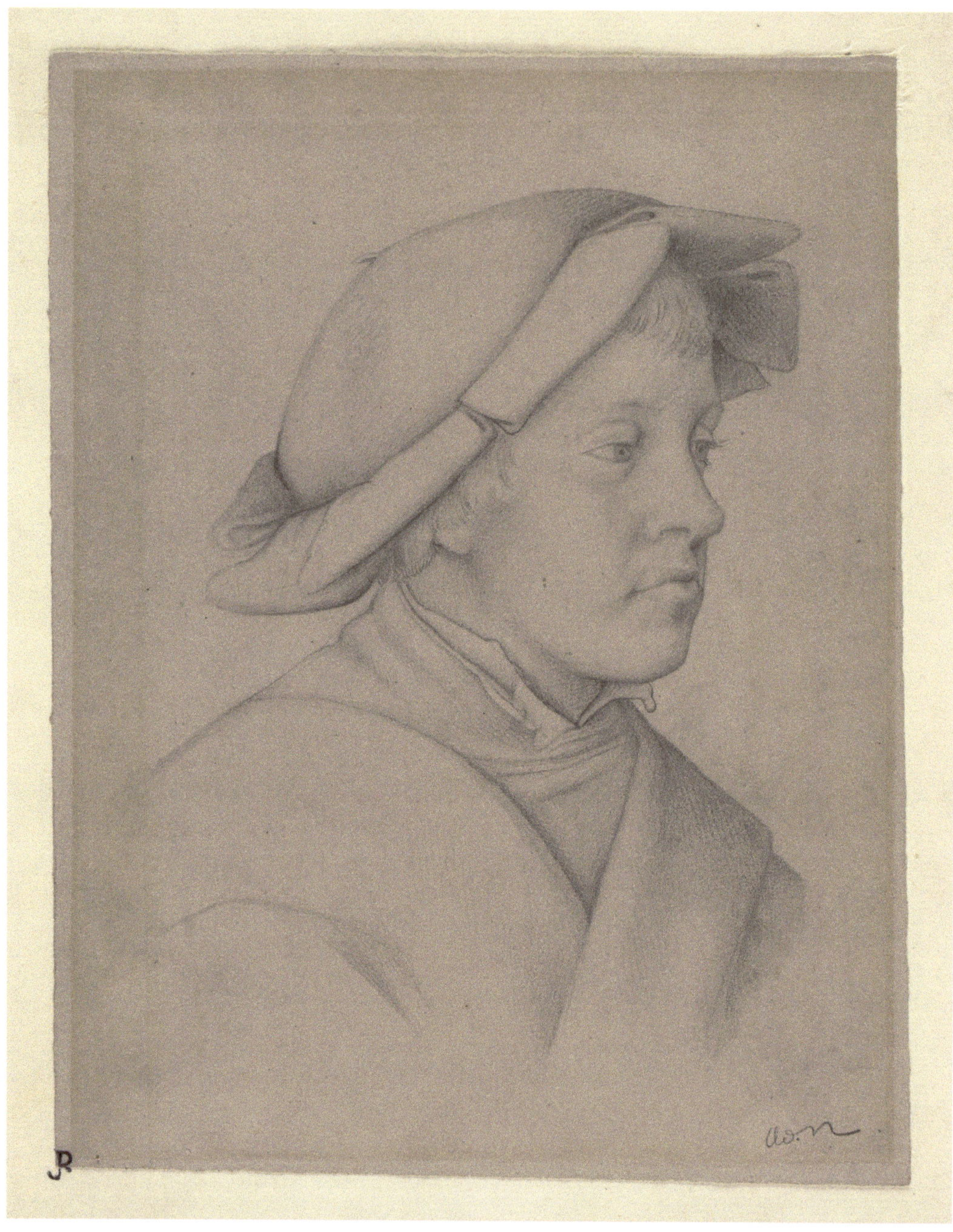

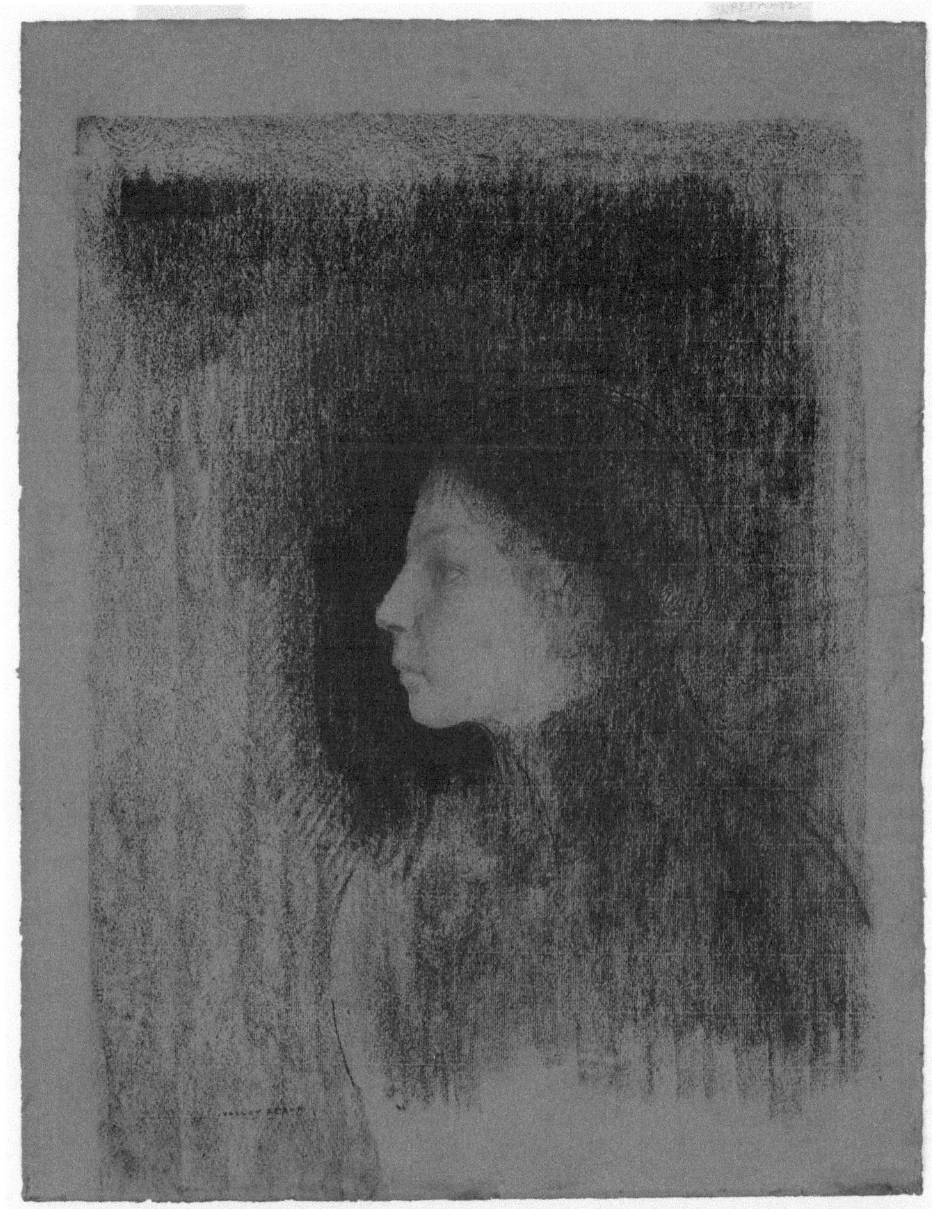

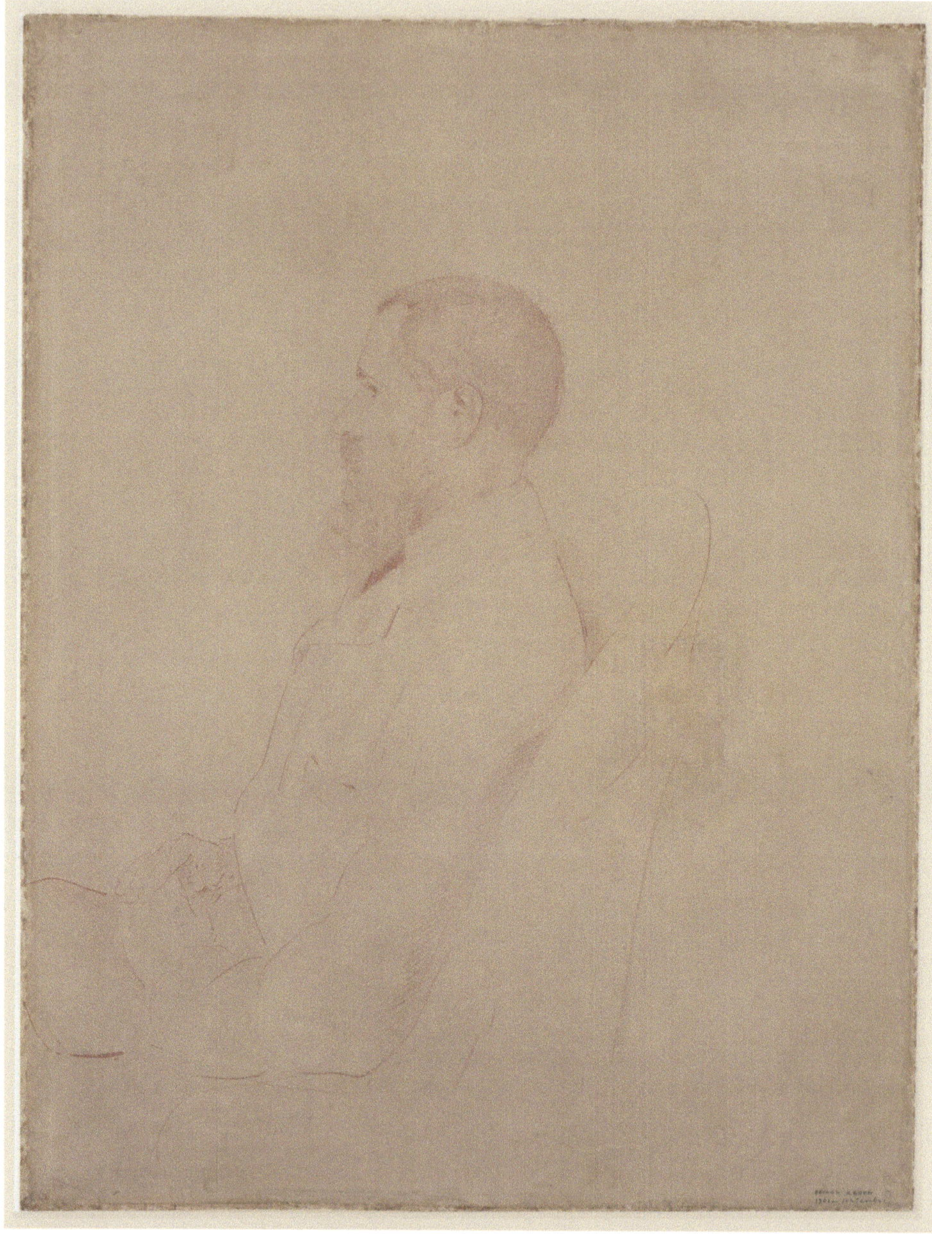

Profile of a Woman

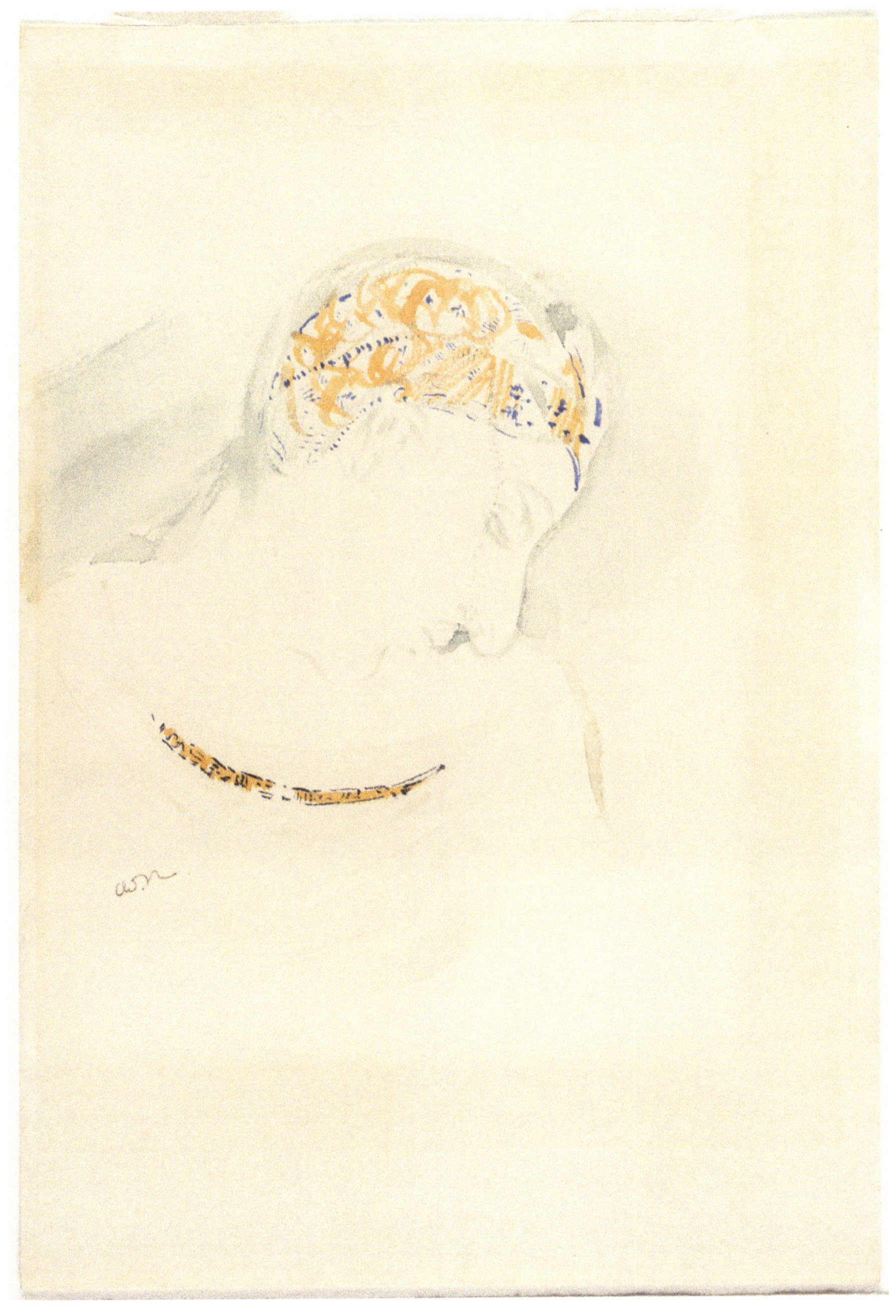

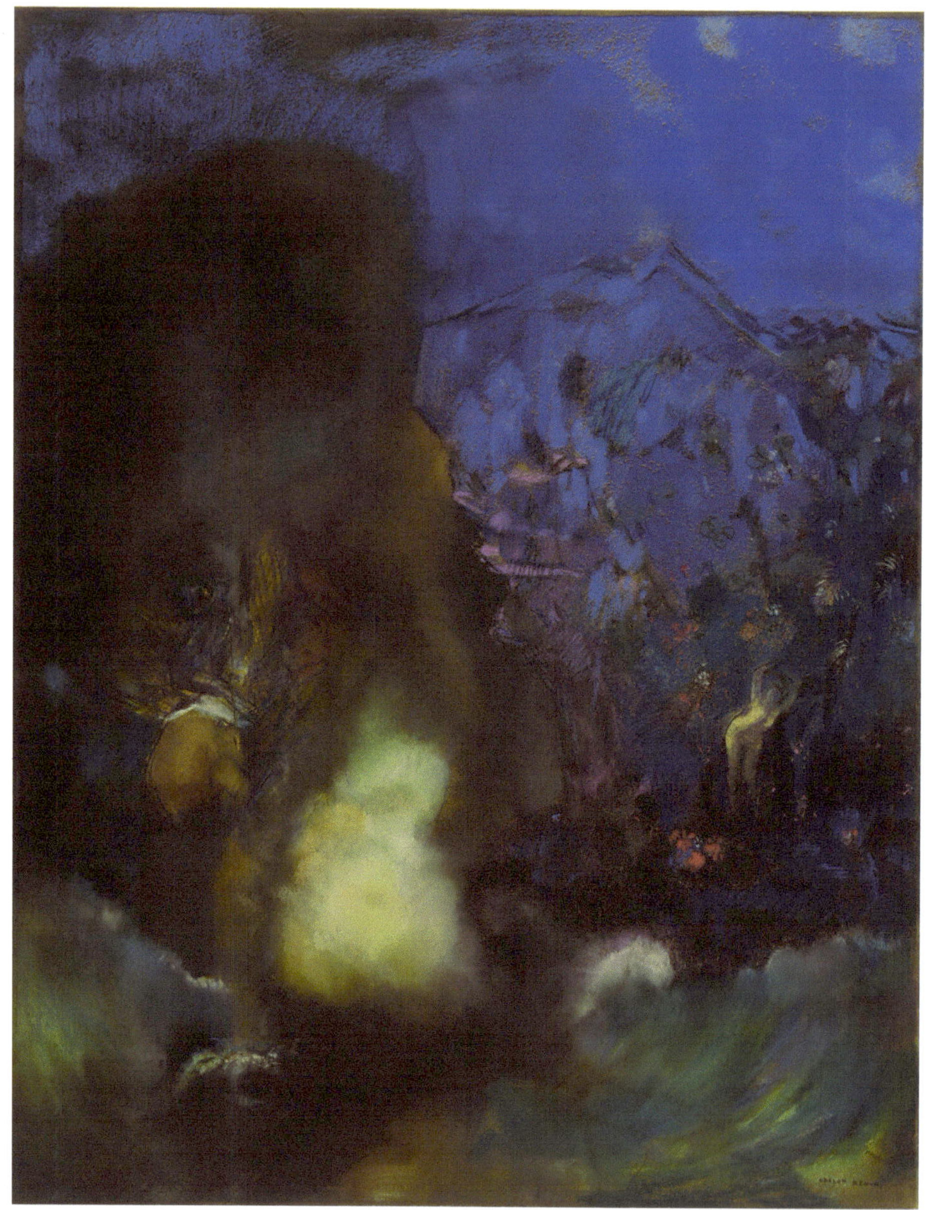

92.7 x 73 cm

Museum of Modern Art, New York, USA

Silence, 1911

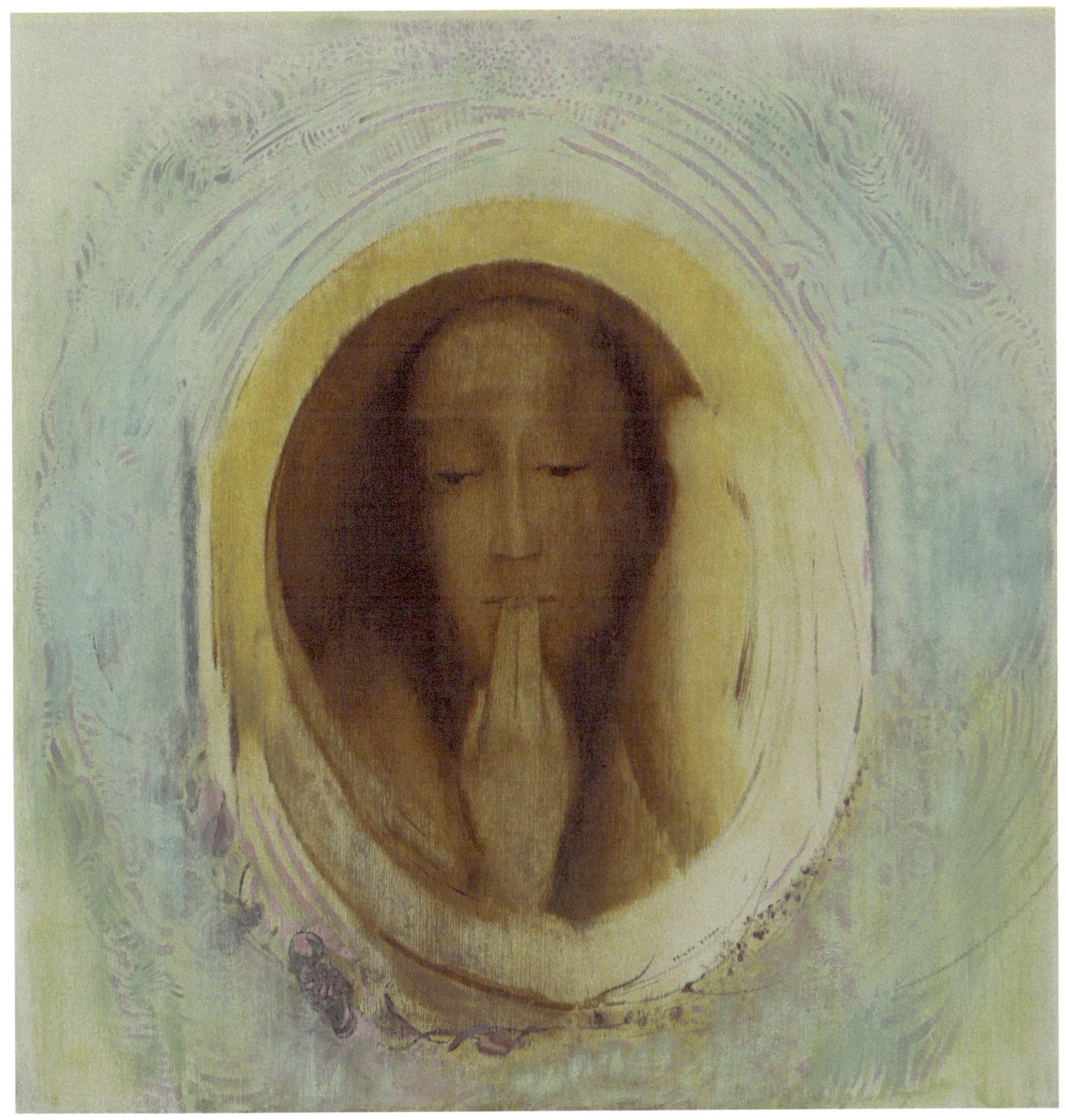

54.6 x 54 cm

Museum of Modern Art, New York, USA

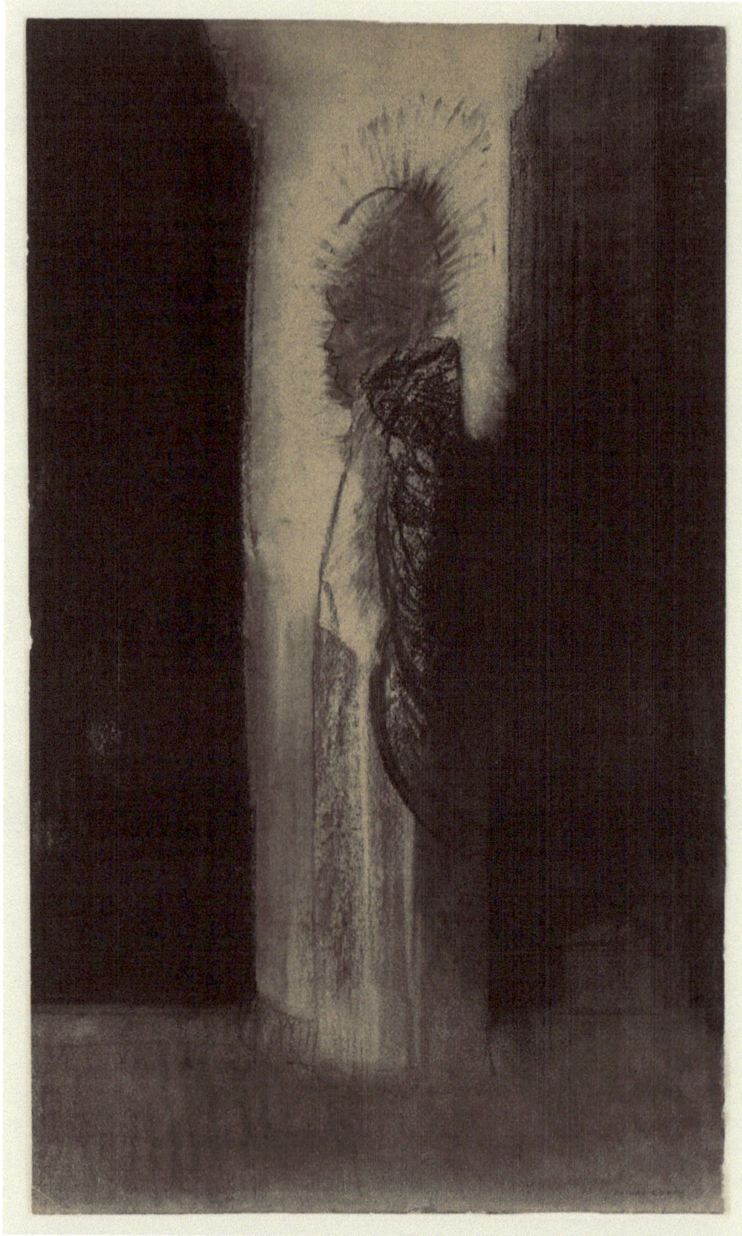

The Barque, 1902

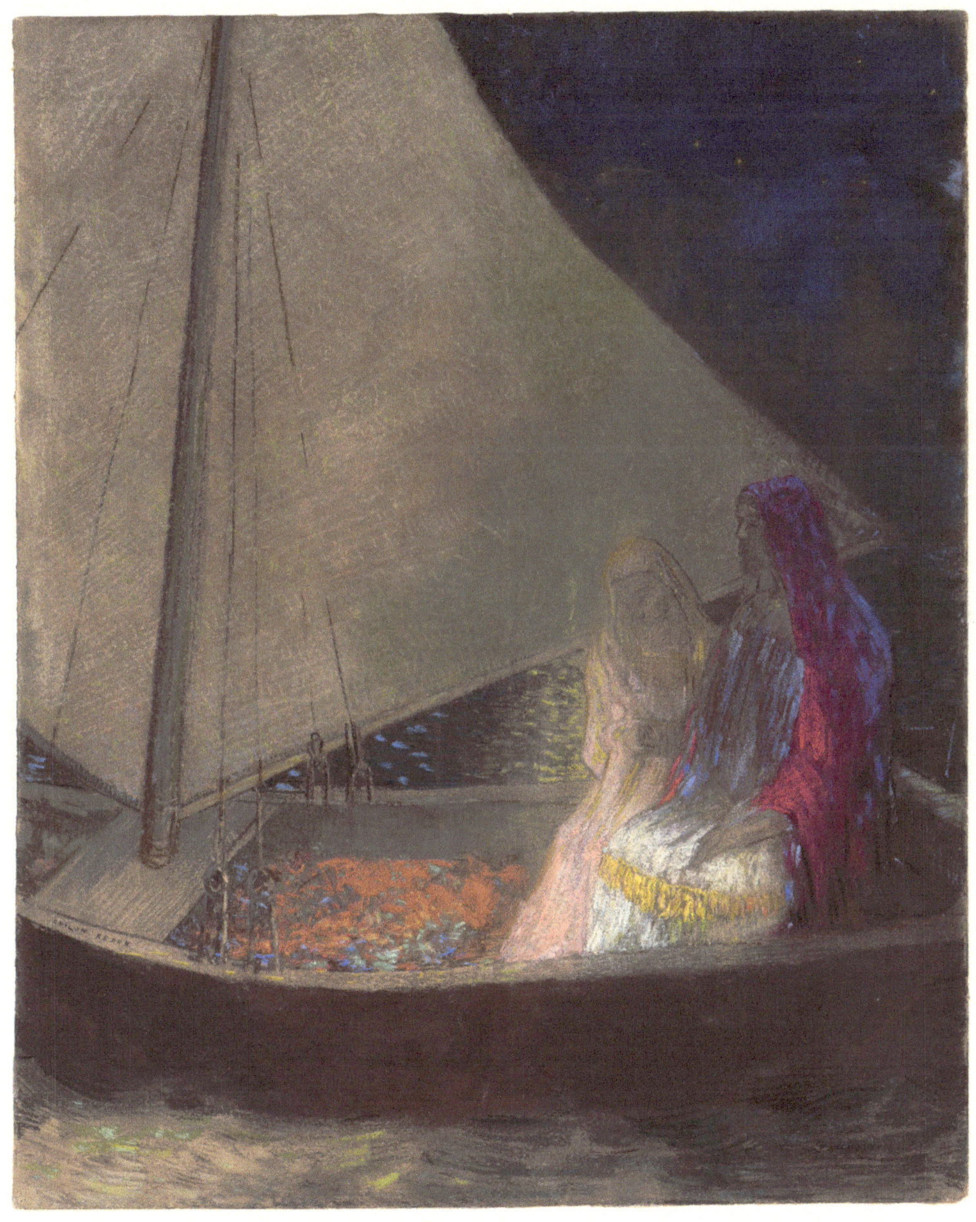

61 x 51 cm

Private Collection

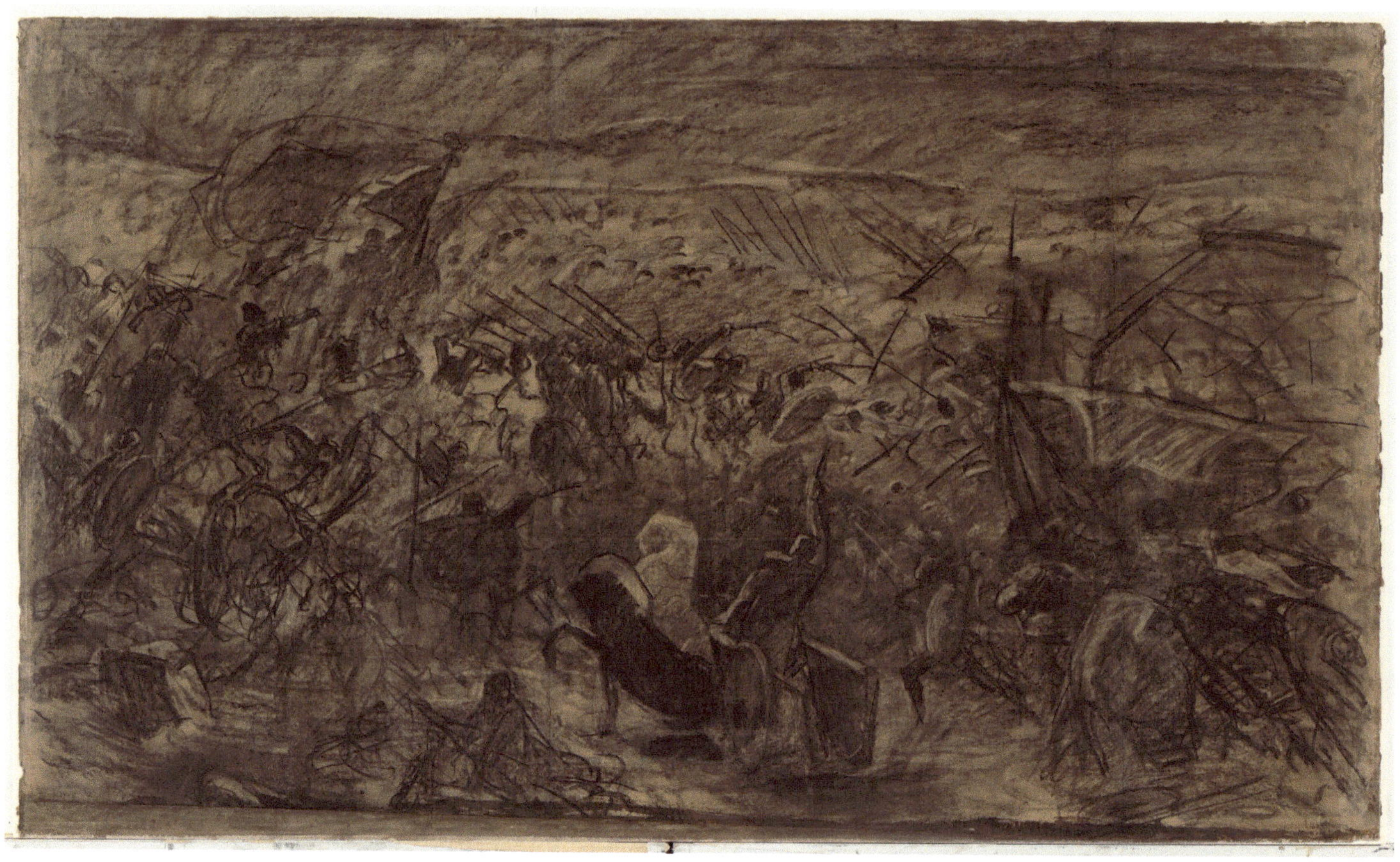

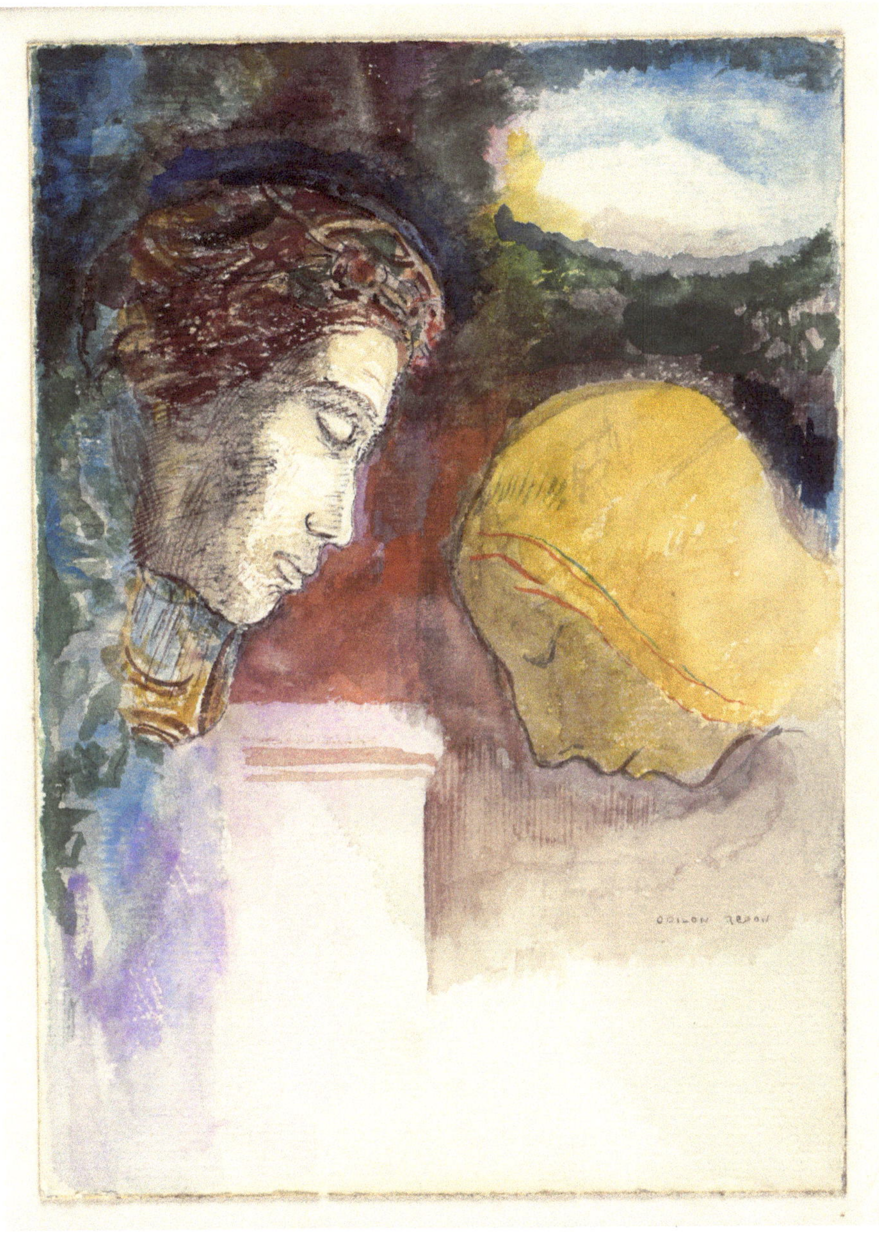

Private Collection

The Blue Vase, c.1910-12

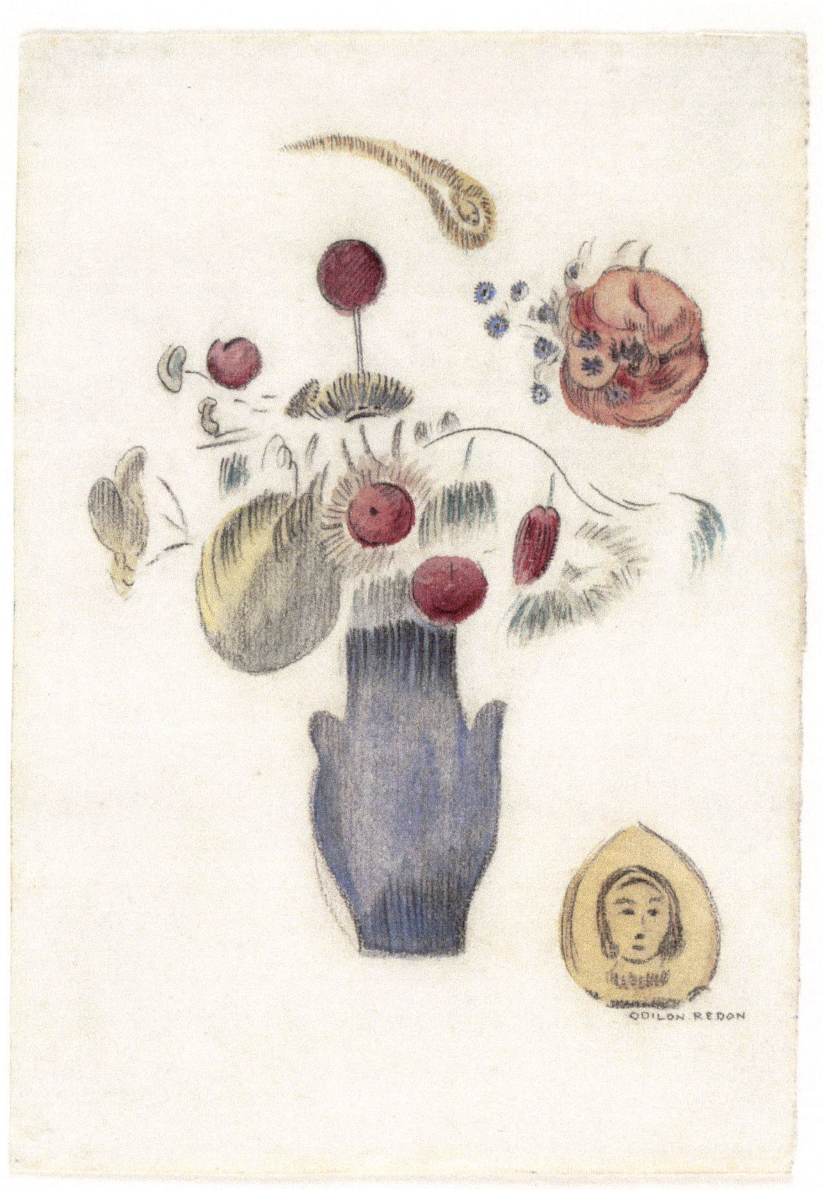

21 x 16 cm

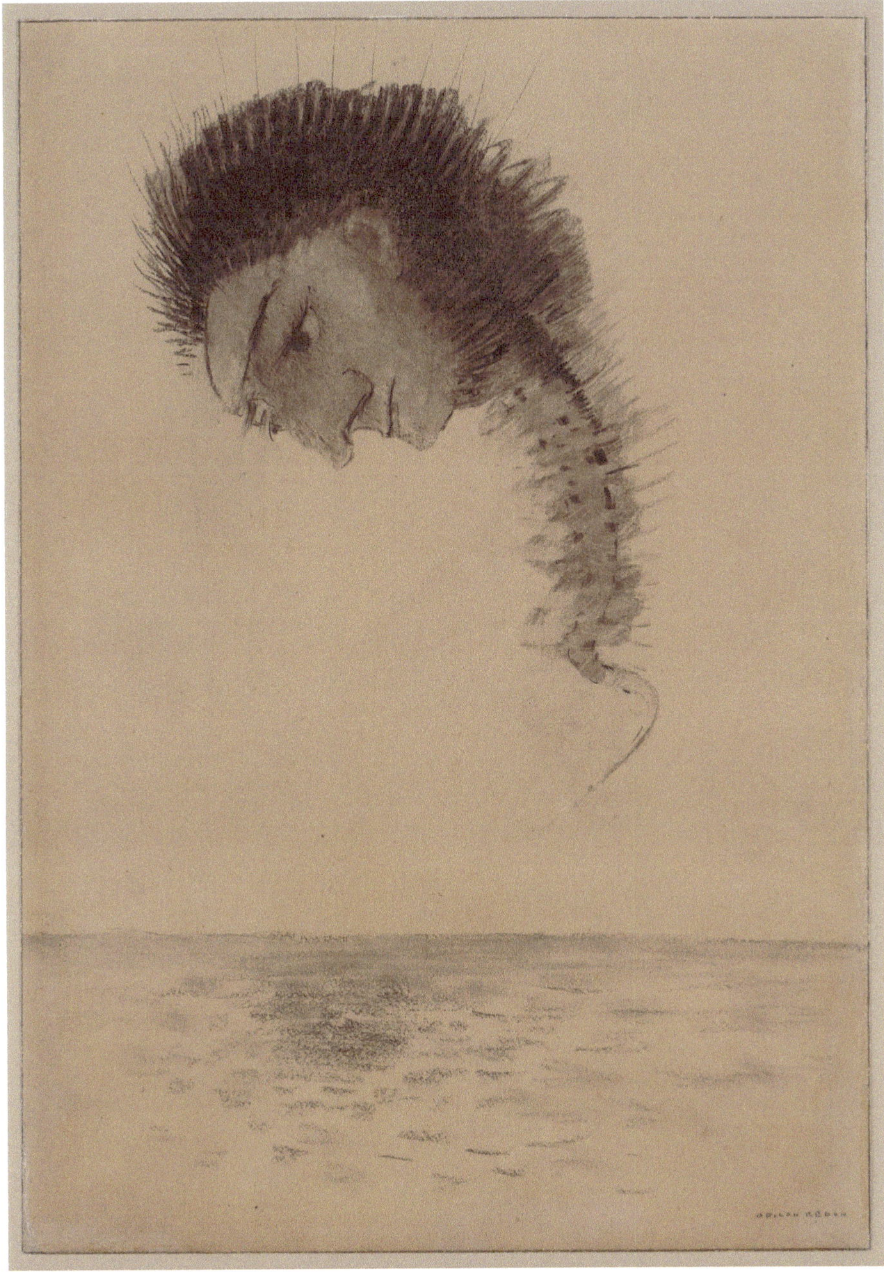

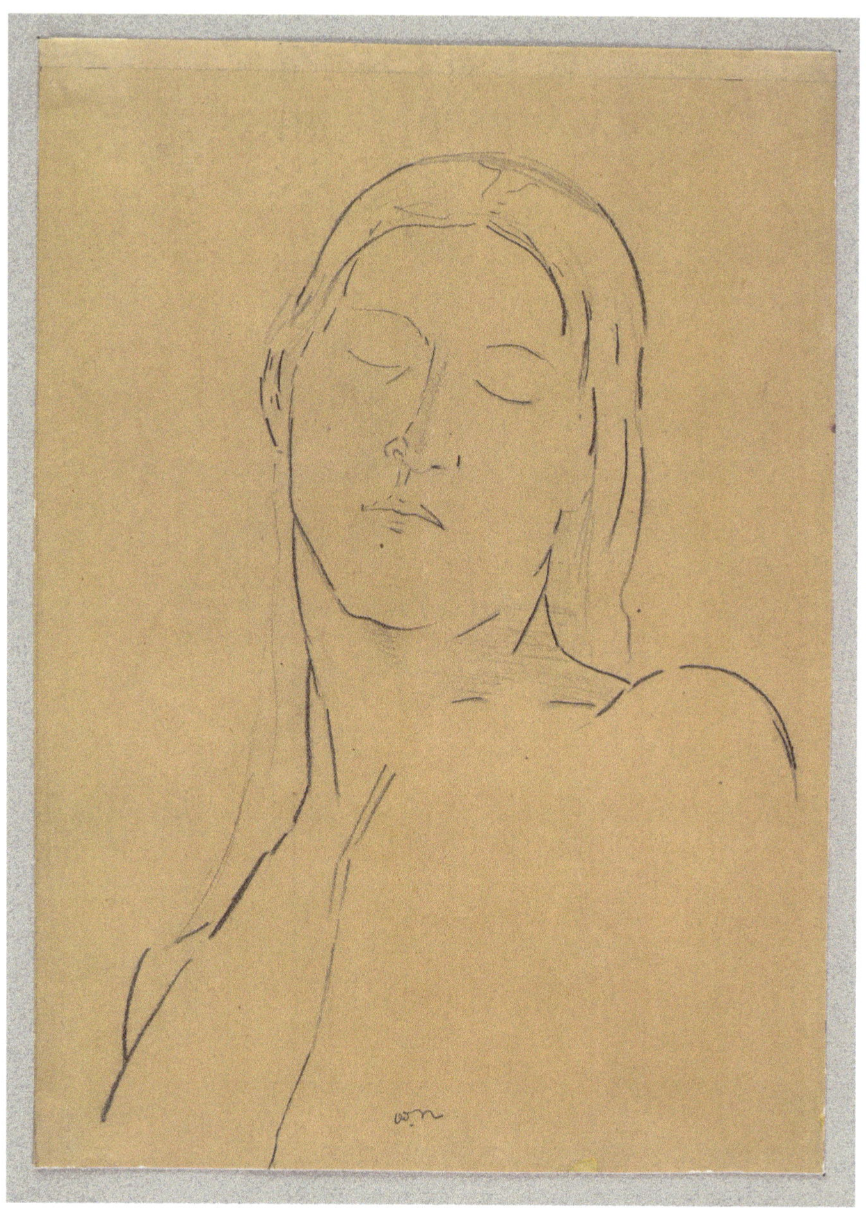

The Convict, 1881

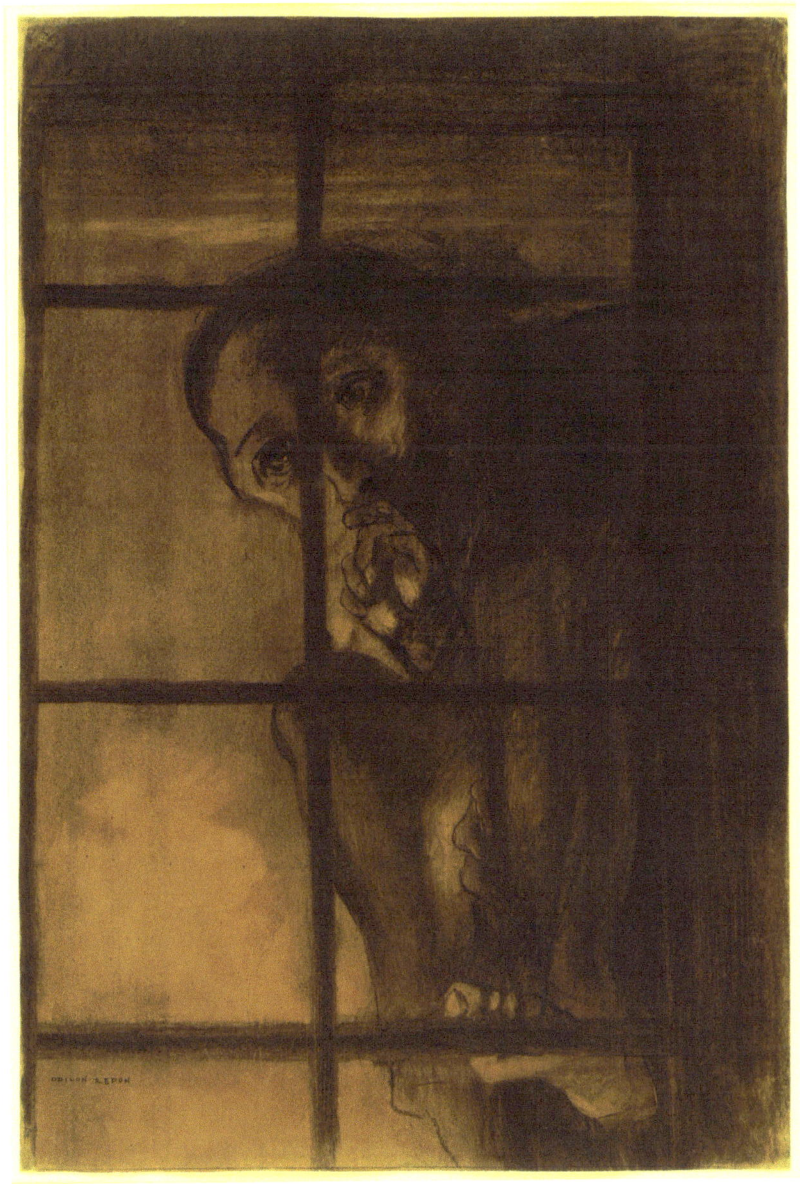

Museum of Modern Art, New York, USA

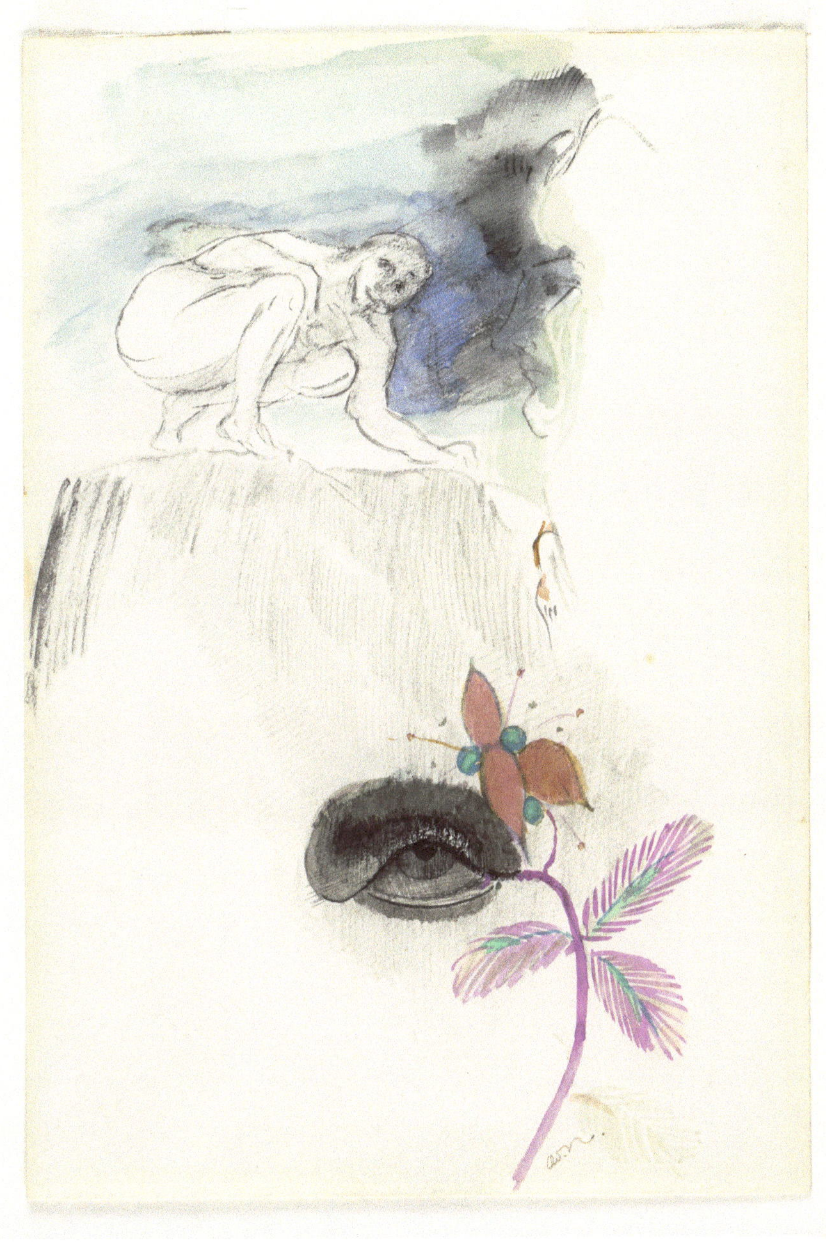

The Fairy, 1886

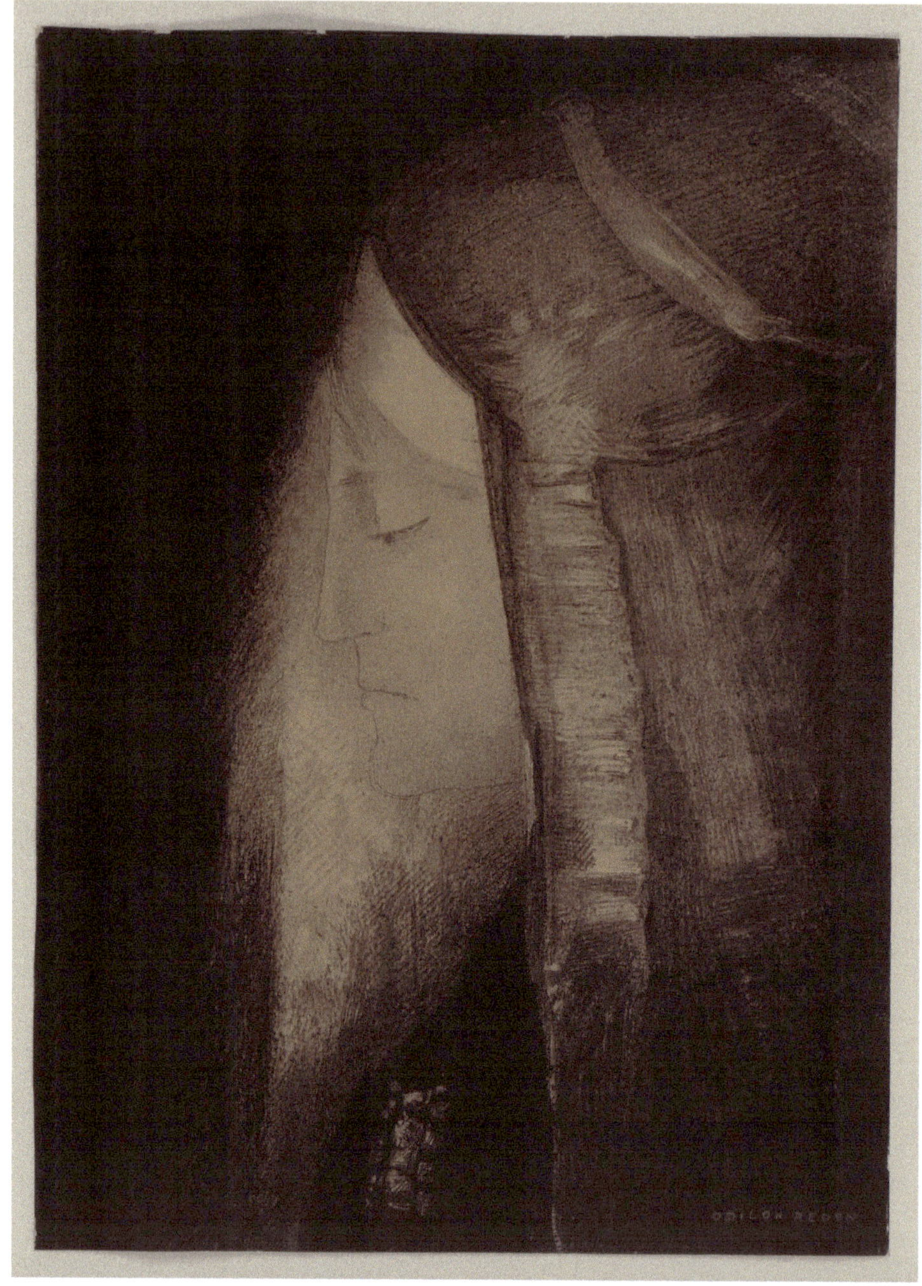

45 x 35 cm

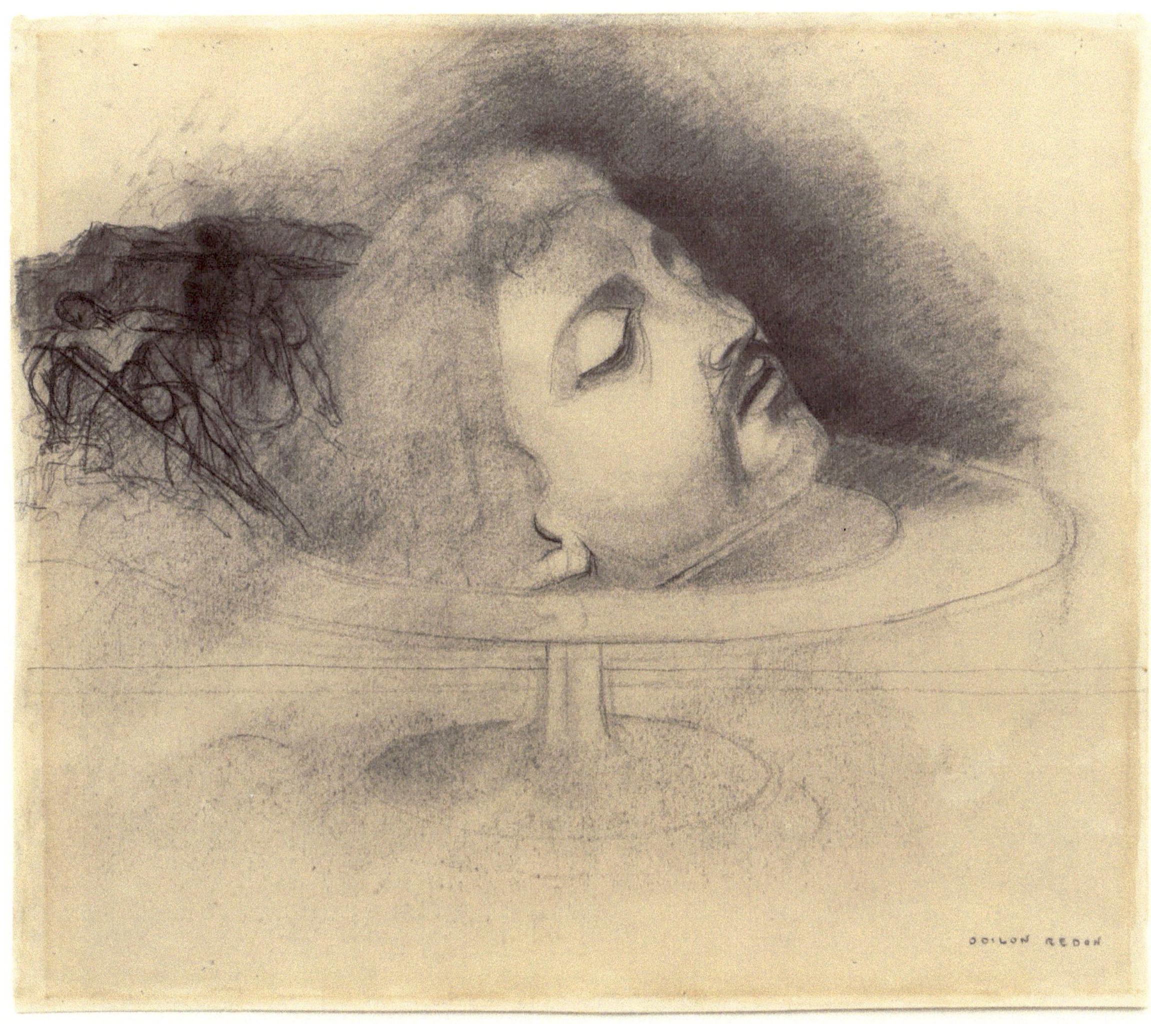

29.2 x 34 cm

The Masque of the Red Death, 1883

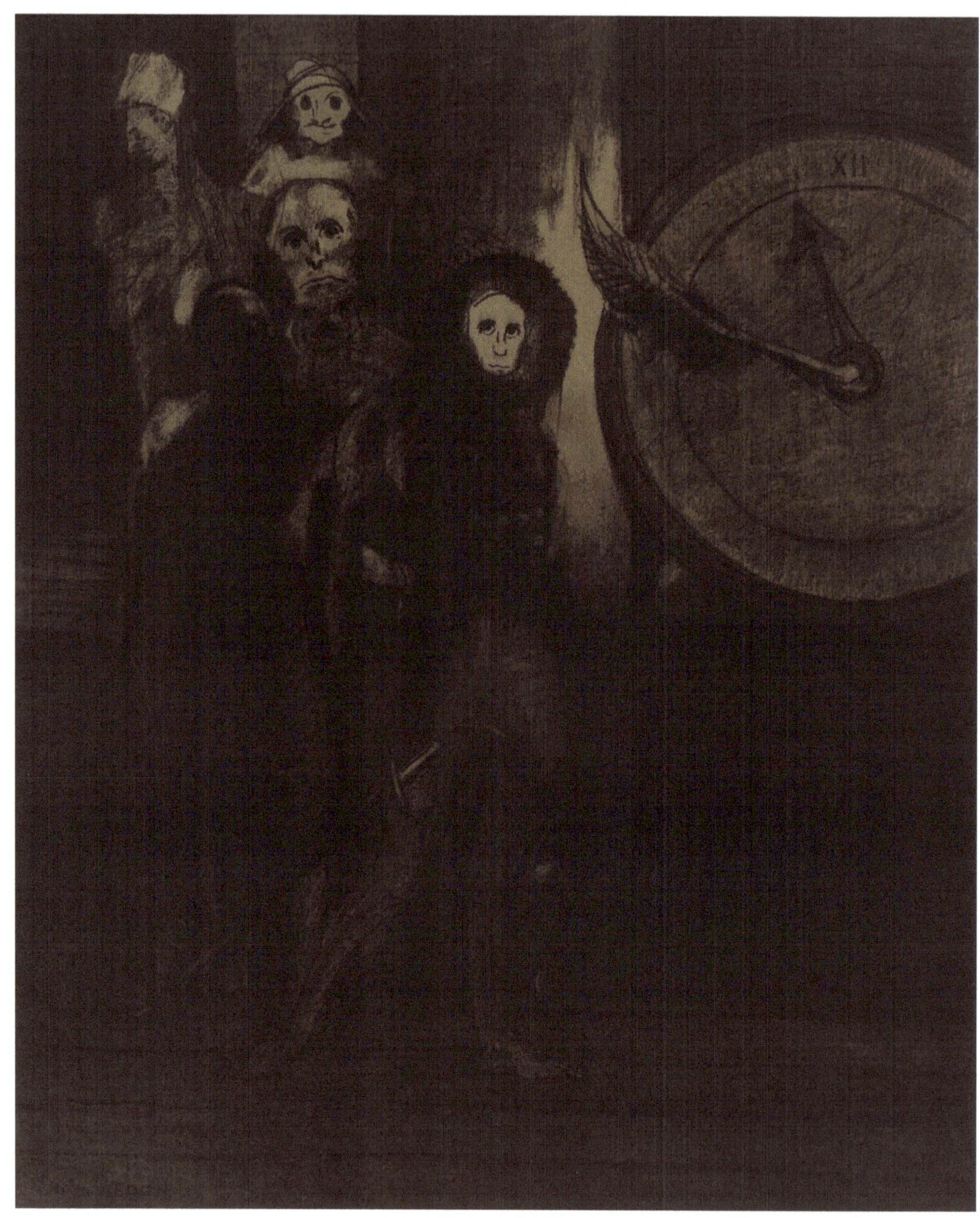

Museum of Modern Art, New York, USA

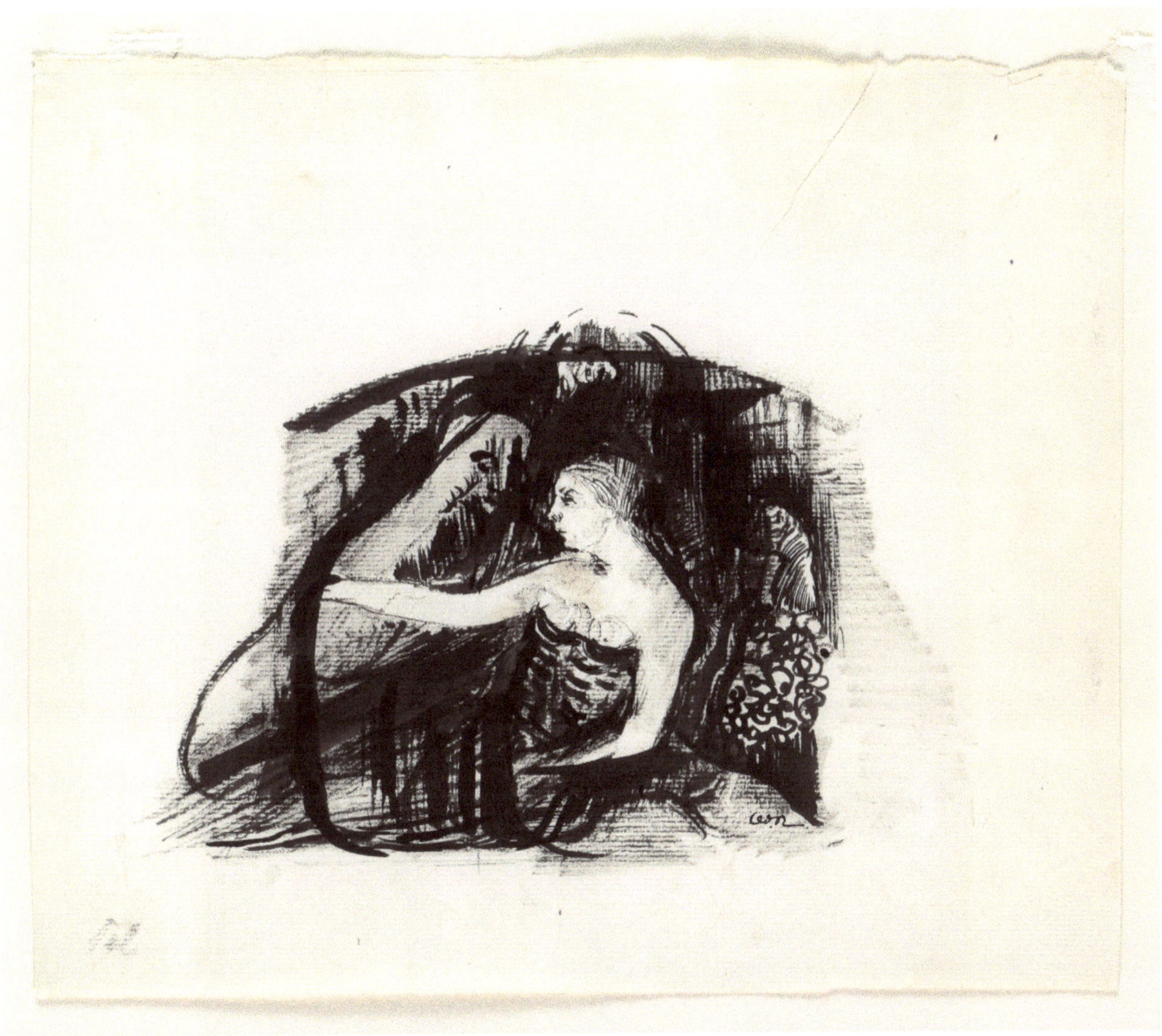

The Teeth, 1883

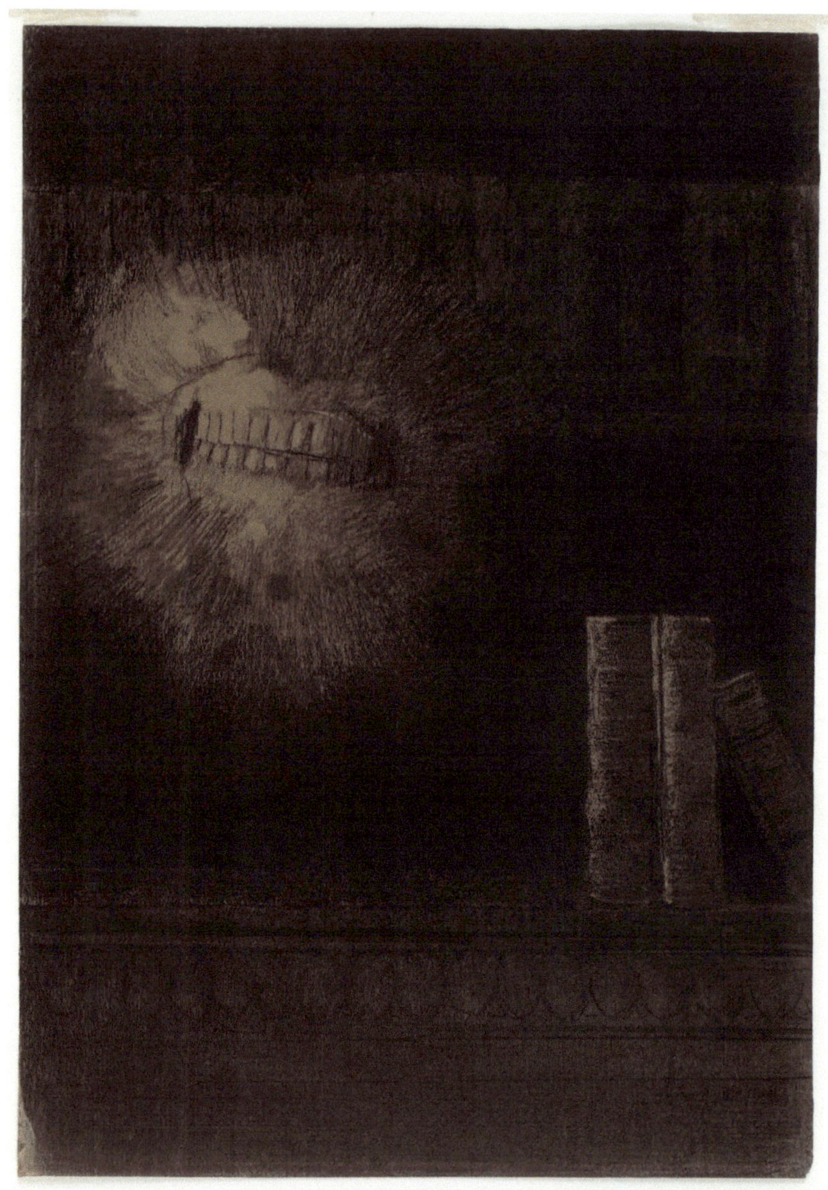

51.1 x 36.8 cm

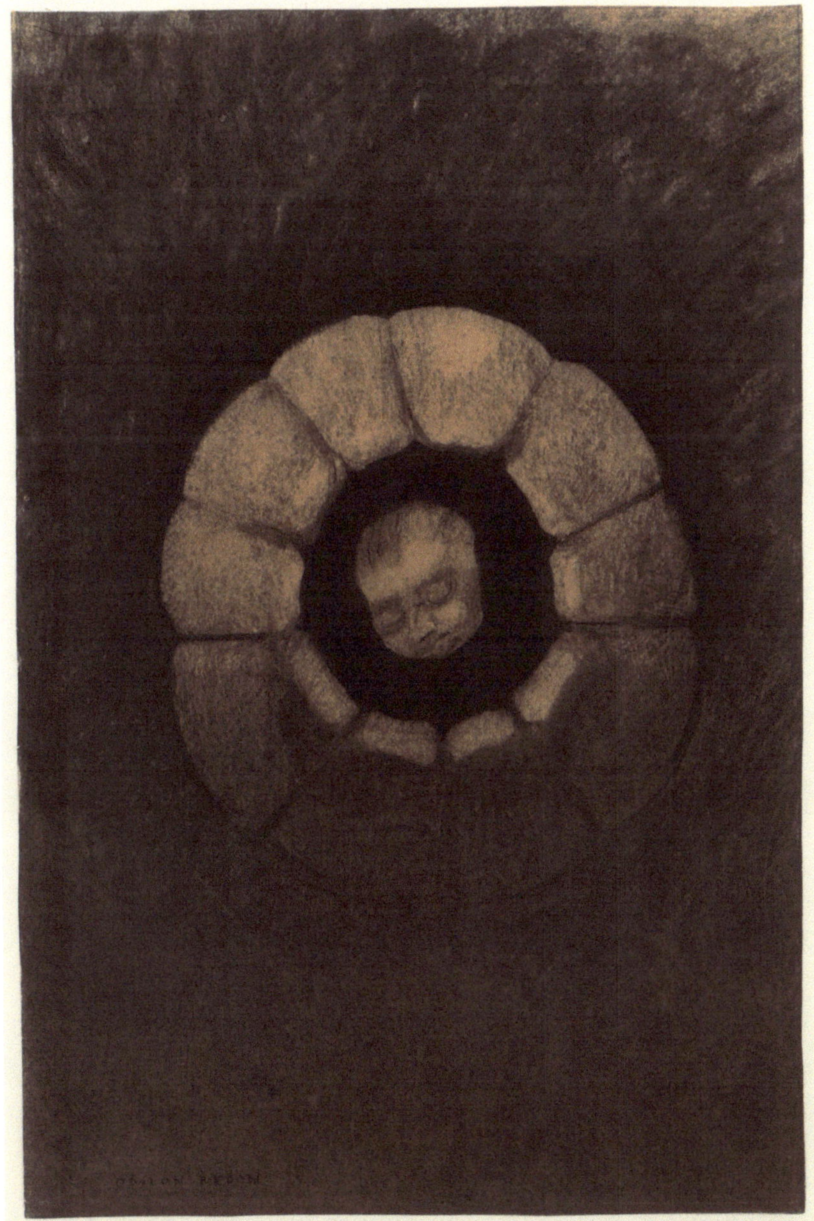

35.6 x 23.8 cm

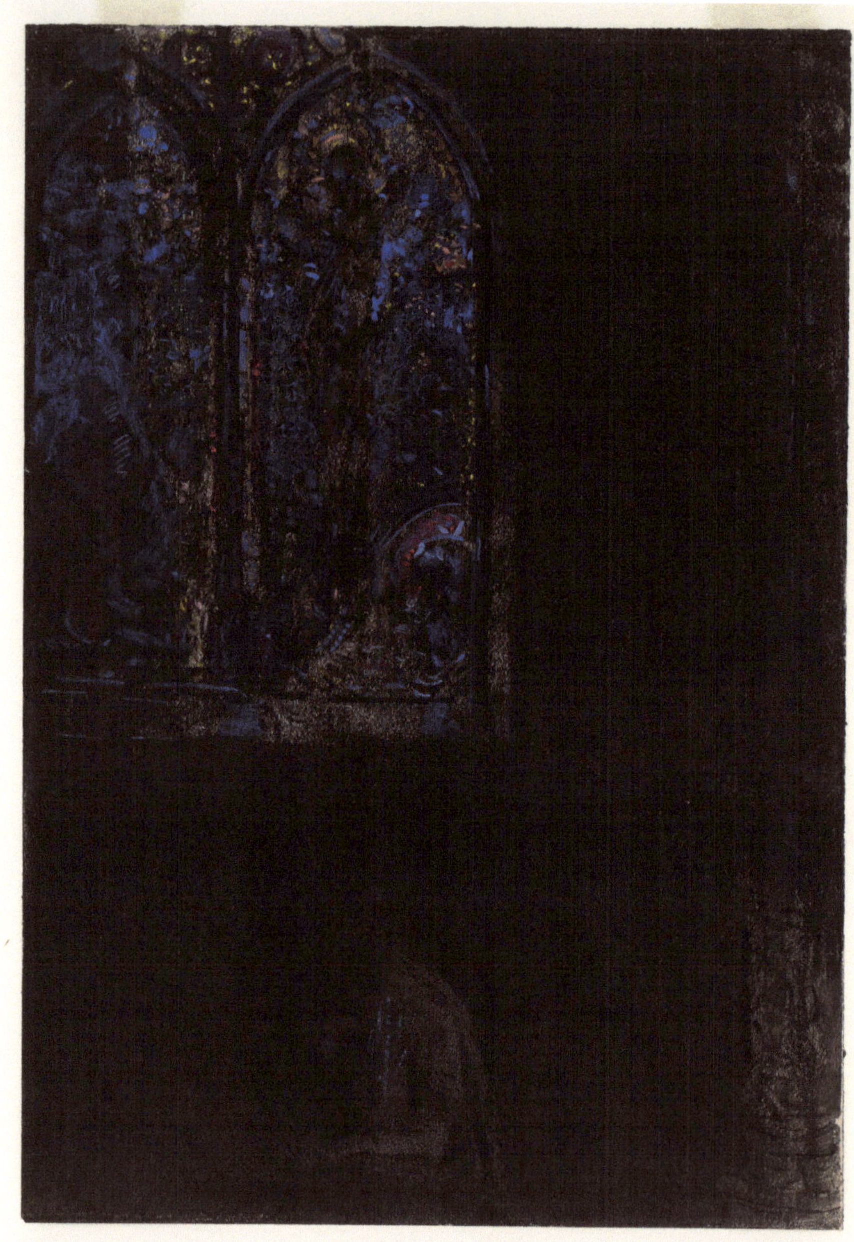

Through the Crack a Death's-Head Was Projected, c.1886

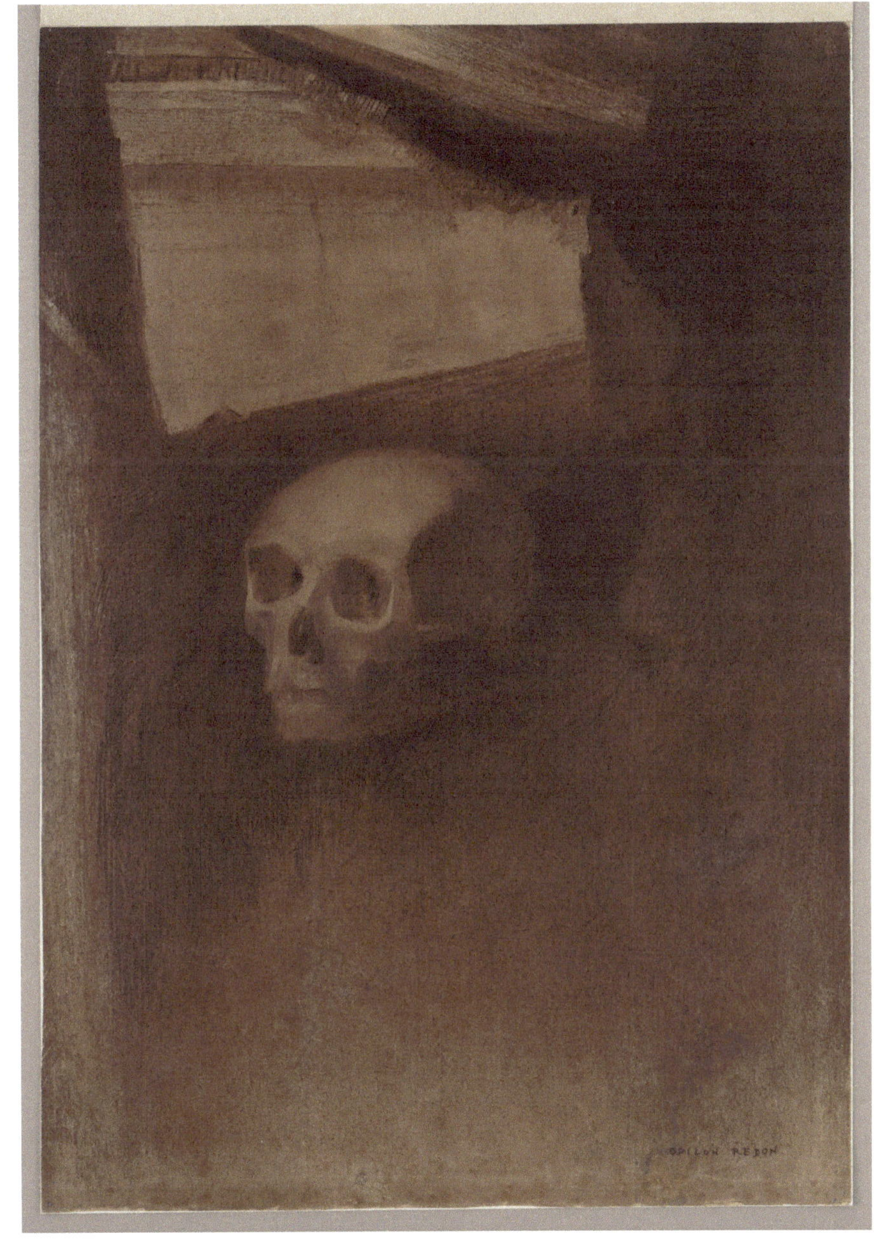

Vase of Flowers, c.1905

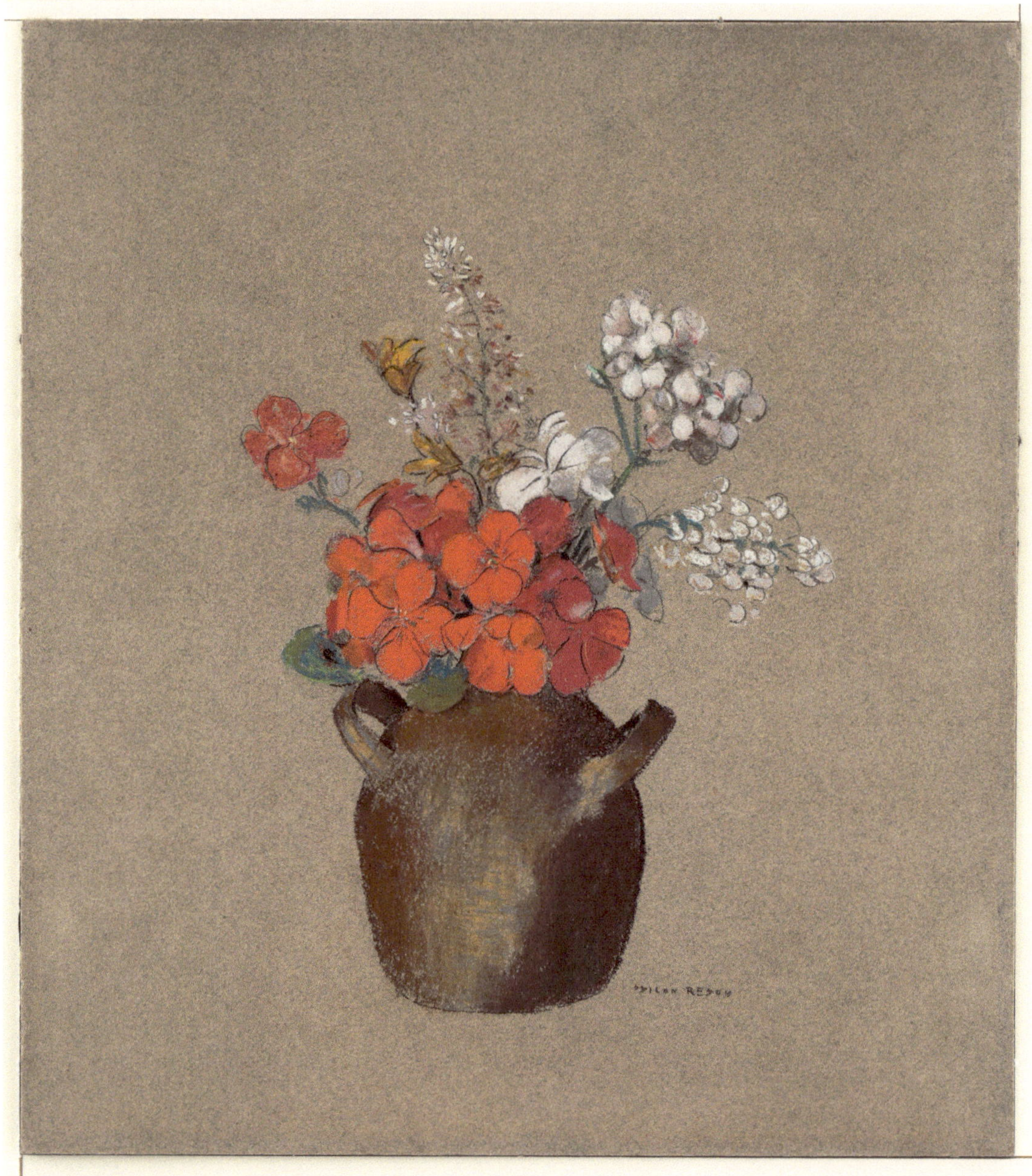

41.3 x 37.8 cm

Museum of Modern Art, New York, USA

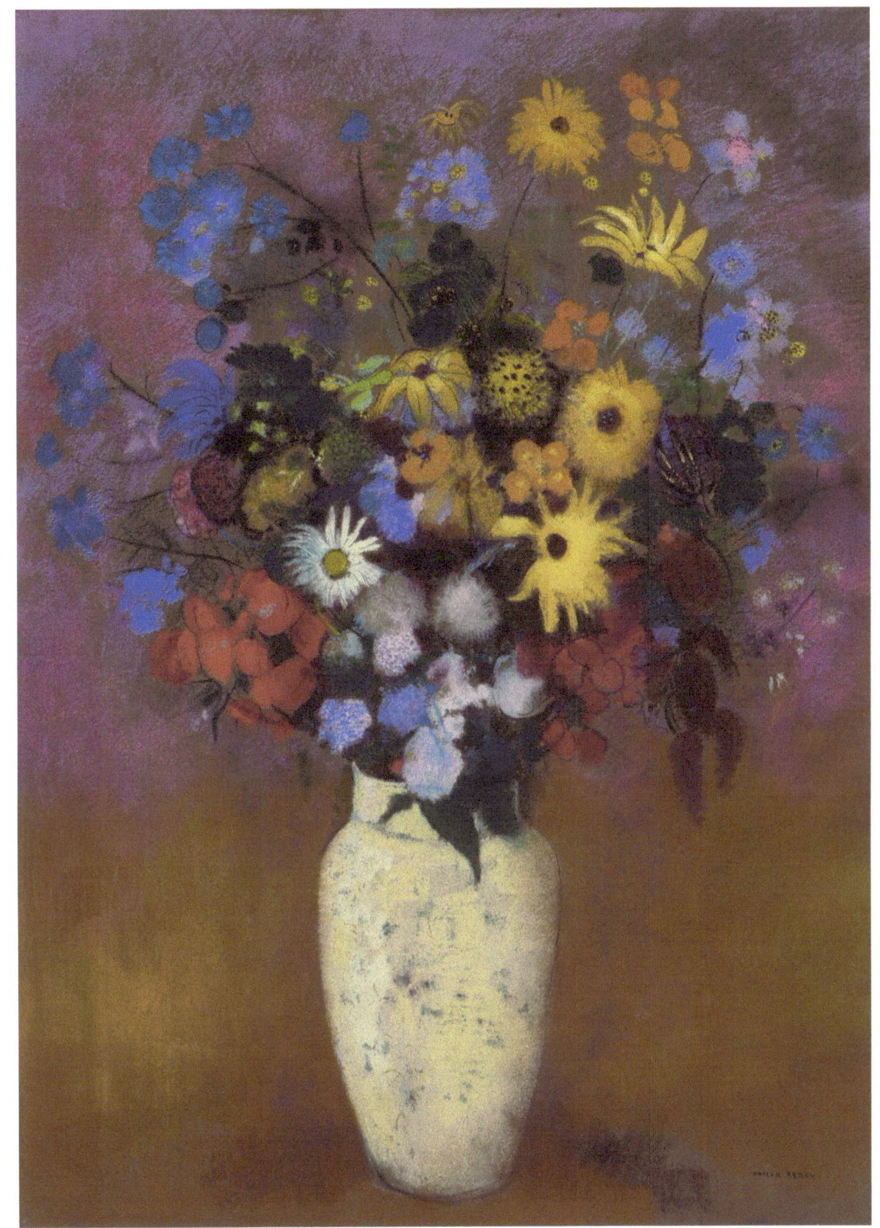

73 x 53.7 cm

Museum of Modern Art, New York, USA

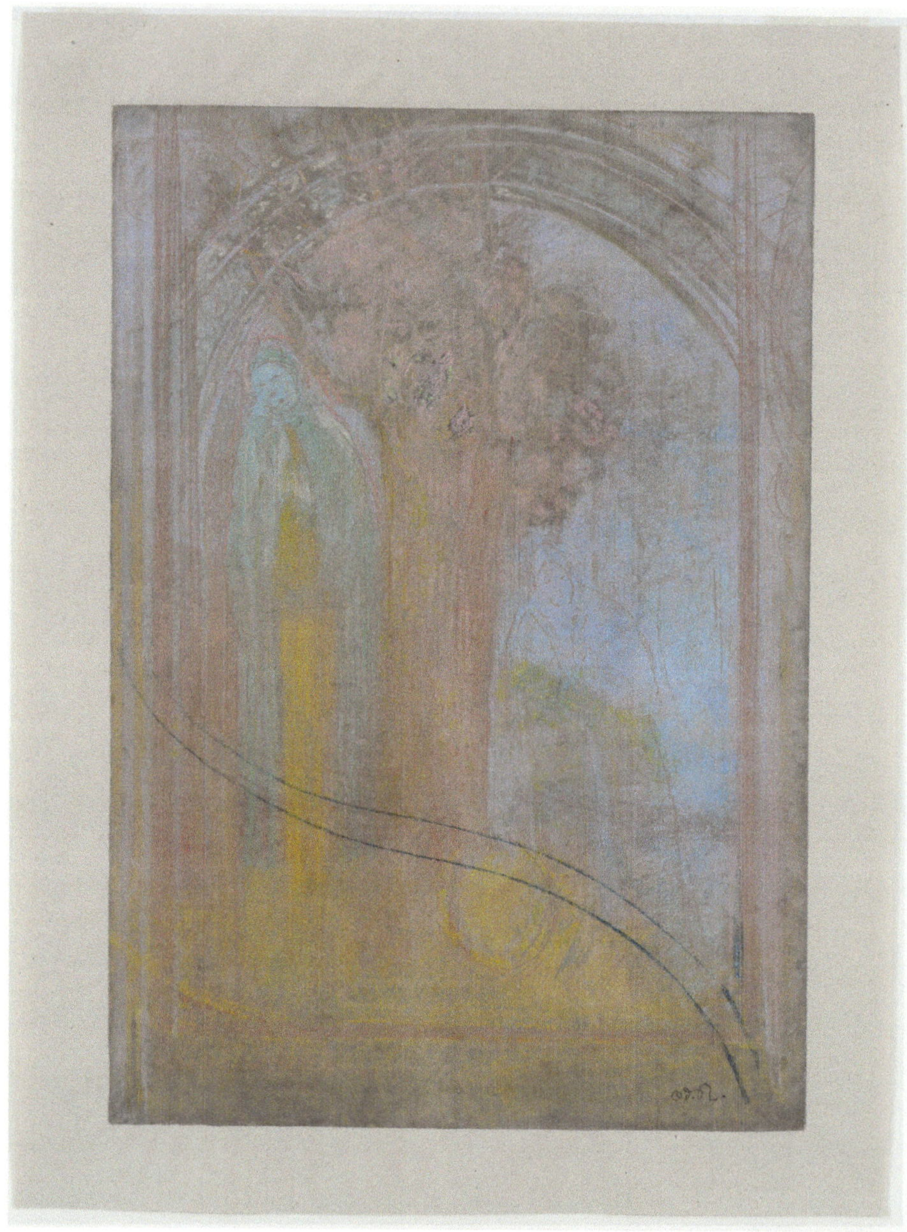

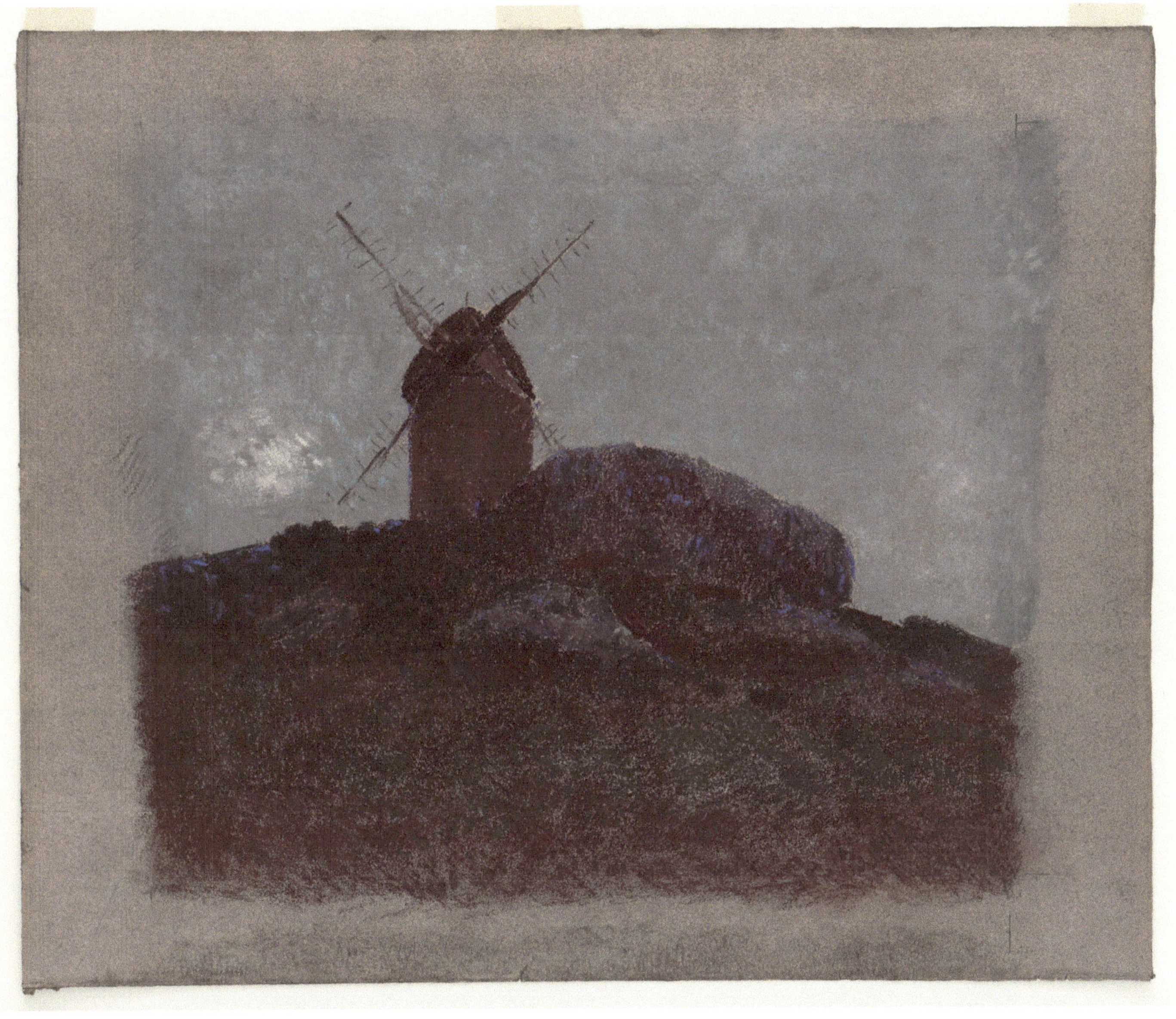

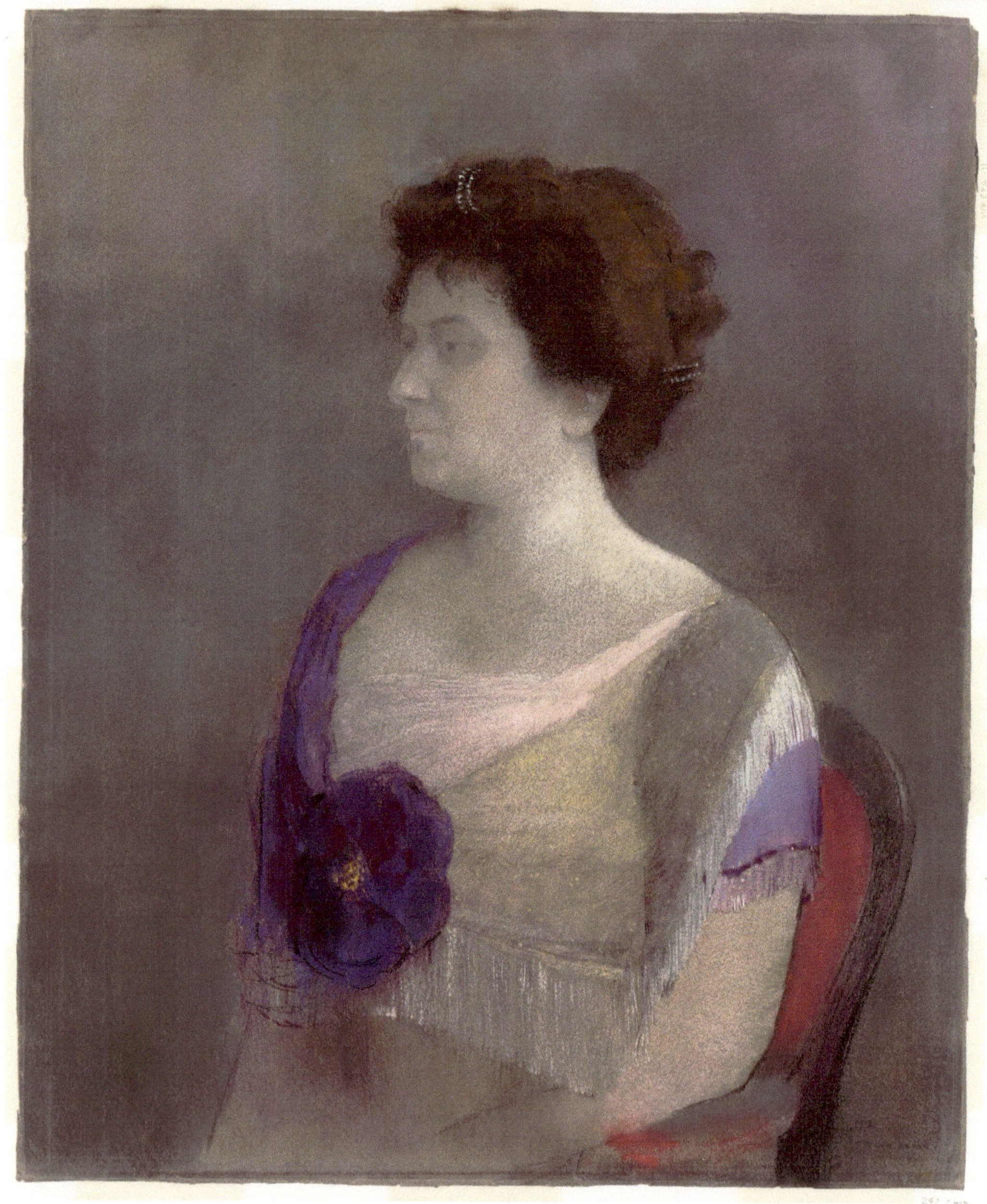

Paul Klee, 1879~1940

Paul Klee was born on December 18, 1879, in Münsingen, near Bern, Switzerland. From a young age, he demonstrated exceptional talent in both painting and music, particularly excelling as a violinist. The inspiration he drew from classical composers such as Richard Wagner, Richard Strauss, and Mozart soon translated into his painting. He aimed to express the complexities of his inner world through abstract forms and symbols, moving beyond mere imitation of reality.

In 1911, Klee became a founding member of the artist group Der Blaue Reiter (The Blue Rider), contributing to the development of abstract painting through elements of symbolism and mysticism. By 1920, he was teaching at the Bauhaus school in Weimar, where he played a crucial role in advancing modern art theory. His experimental approaches and theories significantly influenced future generations of artists.

With the rise of the Nazi regime, the Bauhaus was dissolved in 1933, prompting Klee to return to Switzerland, where he continued his artistic endeavors until his death in 1940. Throughout his life, he created a diverse array of paintings, drawings, and prints.

Paul Klee passed away from acute heart failure on June 29, 1940, in Muralto-Locarno, Switzerland. A photograph taken four months before his death showed him with pale skin and prominent wrinkled lips.

Heroic Strokes of the Box, 1938

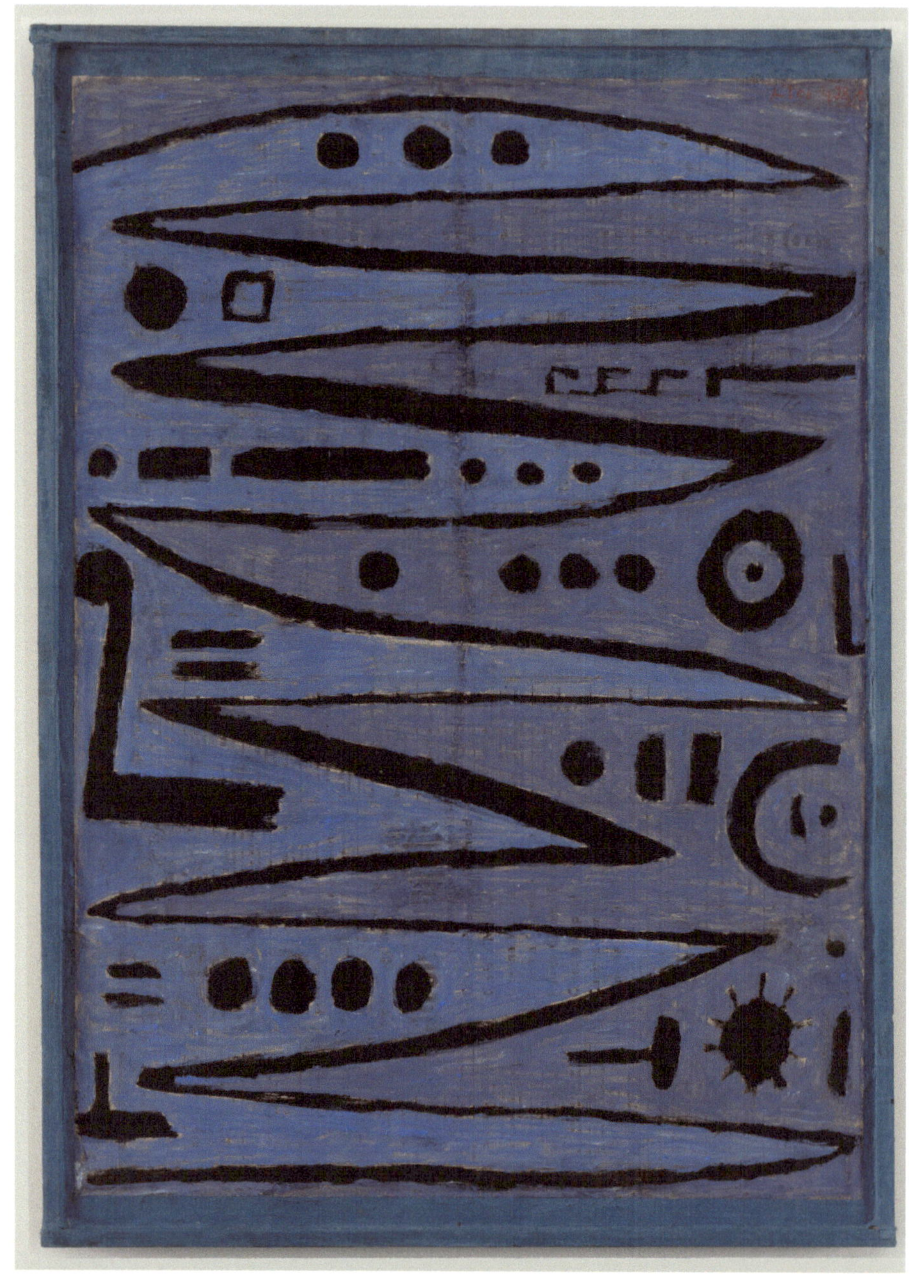

Museum of Modern Art, New York, USA

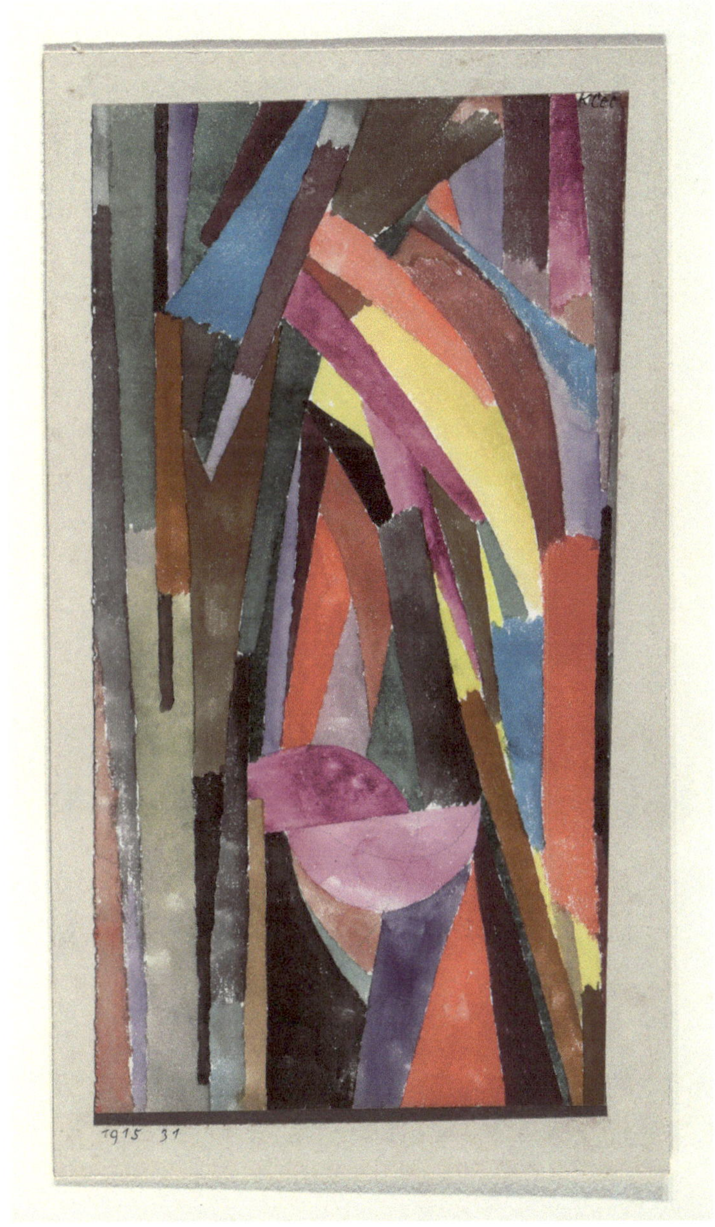

28.9 x 16.5 cm

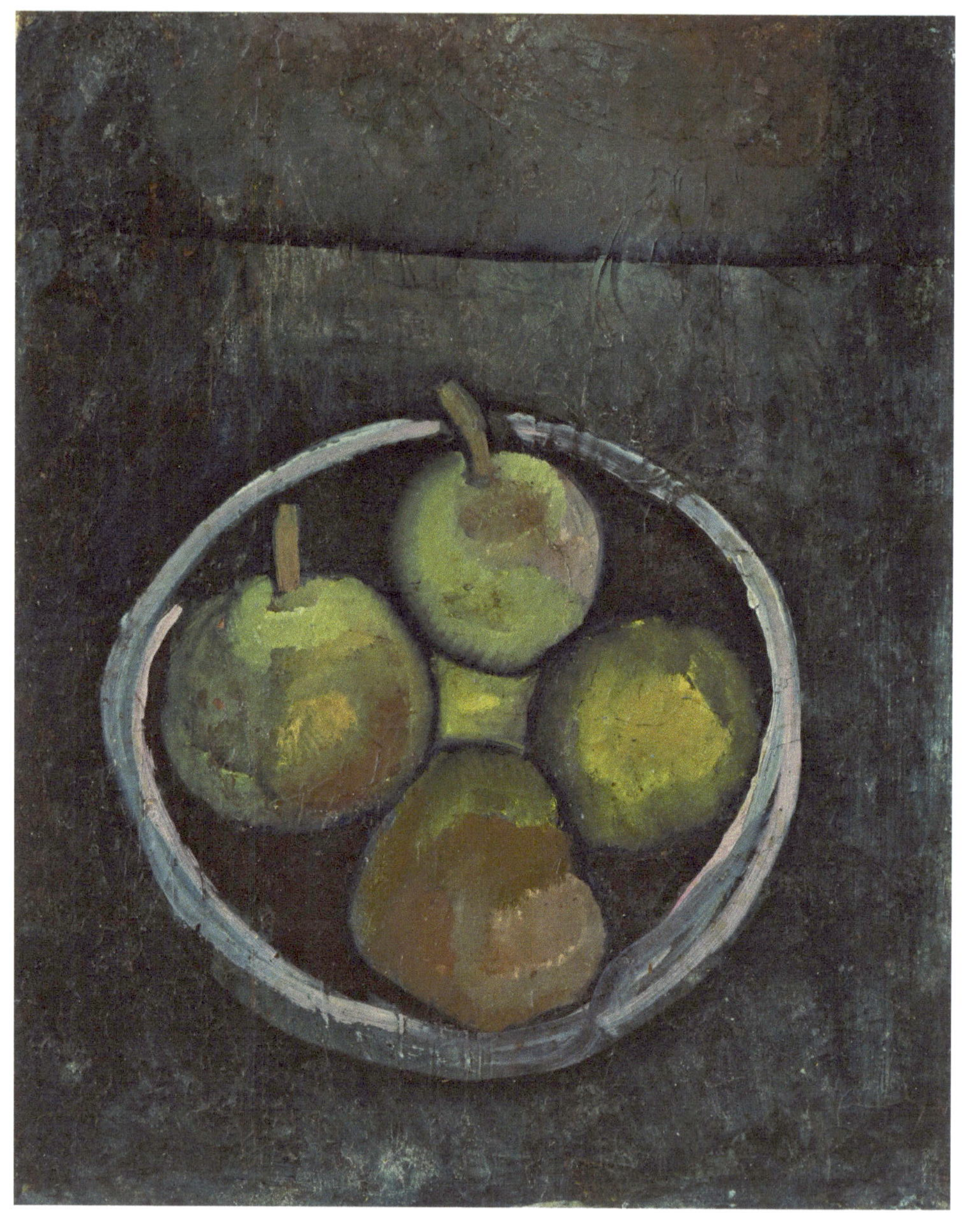

34 x 28 cm

Museum of Modern Art, New York, USA

The End of the Last Act of a Drama, 1920

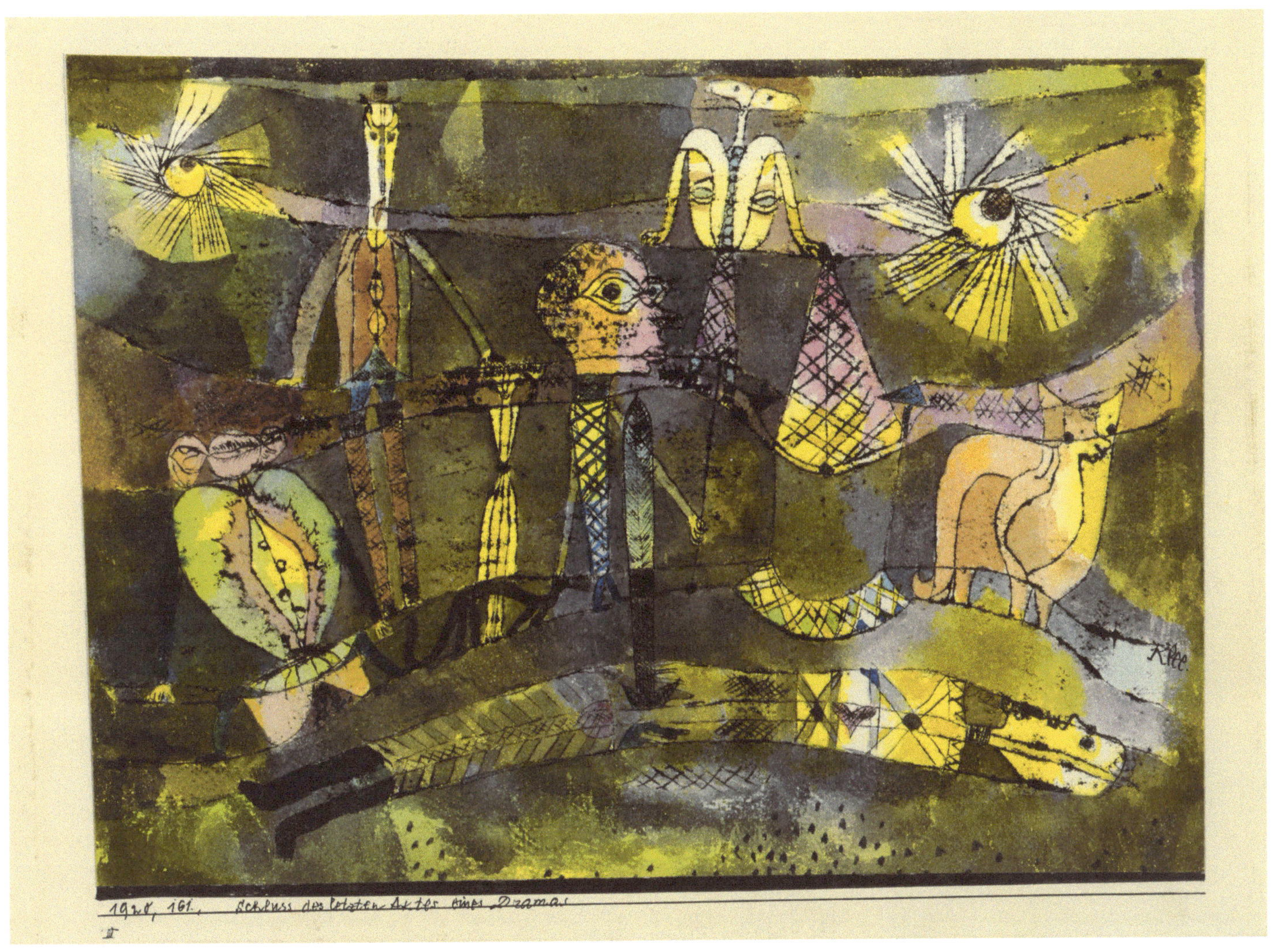

24.1 x 33.3 cm

Sophie Taeuber-Arp, 1889~1943

Sophie Taeuber-Arp was born on January 19, 1889, in Davos, Switzerland. She was a versatile artist active in various fields, including visual arts, sculpture, architecture, and modern dance.

She studied textile design at the School of Applied Arts in St. Gallen, later continuing her studies in Munich and Hamburg. In the 1920s, she worked across multiple media, utilizing modern and geometric forms and patterns, and reinterpreted traditional techniques such as needlepoint embroidery in innovative ways.

Building on her textile craft, she expanded into accessory design, including textiles, clothing, and handbags. Her work as a textile artist is renowned for its geometric patterns and vibrant color combinations. She also created groundbreaking designs for marionettes and stage and costume design. In 1918, her marionette work gained significant attention at the Cabaret Voltaire in Zurich, where she became a key figure in the Dada movement.

In addition to her artistic pursuits, Arp was also active as a modern dancer. She explored new horizons in dance alongside her friends, bringing creativity and originality to her performances. In 1926, she married the German-French painter Hans Arp, and together they collaborated on numerous projects, deeply influencing each other's work. Tragically, she passed away from carbon monoxide poisoning on January 13, 1943, in Zurich, Switzerland.

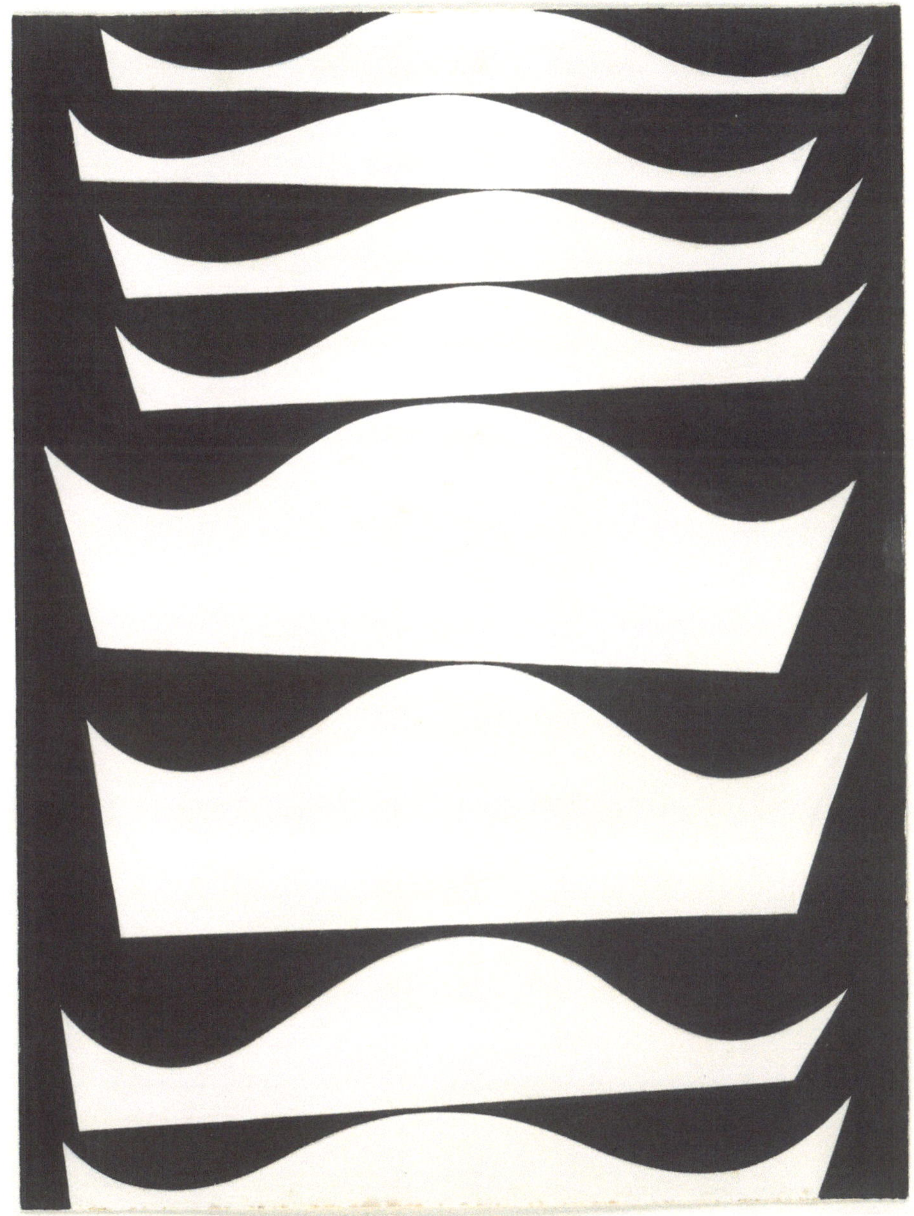

www.ingramcontent.com/pod-product-compliance
Ingram Content Group UK Ltd.
Pitfield, Milton Keynes, MK11 3LW, UK
UKHW060111300726
14090UKWH00002B/131

9791194419037